# Be Smart

## Sail Past the Hazards of
## Conventional Career Advice

First Edition: May 2013

ISBN 13: 978-1483935607
ISBN 10: 1483935604

# Dedication

To our parents, who started us out in life with plenty of advice—most of it good.

To our friends, who can't resist giving us well-intended advice even when we don't ask for it or want it. We sincerely appreciate your insights, mostly listen, and often do what we want to do anyway.

To our clients, who have shared their stories over the years and from whom we have cultivated our own stories captured, in part, in these pages.

To our readers, who might be curious about what we call "conventional career advice" and what advice we are proposing instead. Feel free to take it with a grain of salt and do what you want to do anyway.

*Job security is gone. The driving force of a career must come from the individual. Remember: jobs are owned by the company. You own your career.*

**Earl Nightingale**

# Table of Contents

# Introduction

Whether you are an executive, skilled professional, or recent college graduate, making the right career choices comes with all kinds of challenges, issues, problems, and buried treasures. There's so much riding on your decisions along the way, it's only natural to seek out advice from others.

So, what exactly is "advice?" Here's what authoritative sources say:

>   **ad·vice** *noun* \əd-ˈvīs\ : recommendation regarding a decision or course of conduct : counsel *(Merriam-Webster)*; guidance or recommendations concerning prudent future action, typically given by someone regarded as knowledgeable or authoritative *(Oxford Dictionaries)*

As professional career coaches and consultants for many years, we frequently work with clients who have received well-intentioned advice from family, colleagues and friends about the entire range of career or job search issues. Some of this advice comes from "career professionals" who are expected to have a high level of expertise and knowledge. Even more comes from everyone else who has opinions about these matters. And good heavens, the advice is all over the place! What's a person to believe?

The 19th century American humorist, Josh Billings, said, *"Advice is like kissing: it costs nothing and is a pleasant thing to do."* Giving advice is irresistible for most people, even if they don't really know what they are talking about. What's scary, though, is that it can sometimes be difficult to differentiate good advice from bad. It's even more difficult to recognize well-meaning but still bad advice when it's coming from career professionals who are trusted by their clients for wise counsel.

The world of job search and career management has evolved radically in the past 10 years. The explosion of social media and Internet visibility along with economic upheavals in the last few years have changed nearly everything. In 1997 Daniel Pink, bestselling author of four books on how the world of work is changing, described the job world we live in as the "Free Agent Nation," a world in which workers are not tied to organizations in traditional ways. This kind of environment has had a more profound impact on employee behaviors and expectations than he probably imagined at the time.

What we hope to accomplish in this book is to challenge assumptions, rattle cages, and shake the trees of conventional "wisdom." We don't claim to be "right" necessarily, but we have worked with thousands of clients—employees, job seekers, professionals in career transition—and we are constantly shocked and disturbed by the stories we hear from them. We do have some relatively new approaches and thoughts about what works in today's employment climate.

We've compiled our "new thinking" on pertinent career topics into five primary areas for you to contemplate:

- About Planning: Career and Job Strategies
- About Marketing: Resumes and Collateral Material
- About Visibility and Access: Networking
- About Sales: Interviewing
- About Money: Offer Negotiation and Compensation

We intend to be provocative. We are dedicated to being helpful. If you are able to use just one essay from this book in a way that helps you be successful in your career or job search, then we will have accomplished our goal—helping you sail past the hazards of conventional career advice!

# ABOUT PLANNING:

# CAREER AND JOB STRATEGIES

# Follow Your Dream

CONVENTIONAL WISDOM: Follow your dream. . . do what you love and the money will follow.

NEW THINKING: Follow your dream. . . as long as you factor in reality along the way.

## The Myth

At some point in your career, you'll meet an adviser or consultant who will share the encouraging and supremely optimistic philosophy: "Follow your dream, and the money will follow."

Research shows that the vast majority of people are unhappy in their jobs. There's a good chance you know plenty of people—and maybe you are one of them—who are halfway into their careers only to find that they are not living their dreams. Some people unknowingly call this a mid-life crisis. Should you chuck it all—your job, your degree, your industry, your experience—to follow your passion?

# The Reality

We are optimists and big believers in "doing what you love." Since people spend more time working than doing just about anything else, including sleeping, there's no doubt our jobs should bring us satisfaction and joy. We certainly owe it to ourselves to dream big and follow our dreams.

But if "follow your dream and the money will follow" sounds like a fairy tale, it's because it is. Here's the truth. The further you aim from where you are, what you've been doing, and what you have learned, the more challenging it is to make a change. It can be done, perhaps, but it takes determination, resilience, and a plan. If you want to make a really dramatic change, time is of the essence. It's much easier to shift a career when you're 30 than when you're 50.

In addition, whether you're 30 or 50, the bigger the gap from where you are to where you want to be, the more complicated and risky it is. Imagine that your current existence—location, job, degree, industry, experience—is the epicenter of your career. Let's say, for the moment, that you just want to change location. By staying in your industry, functional role, and professional level, it's relatively easy to move to a different city. Consider now changing your industry *and* your location. You've added a second degree of complexity and risk to the equation. Now consider adding a higher title or position (or higher pay) into the mix. You can understand that the difficulty in achieving these simultaneous goals increases almost exponentially.

In a nutshell, the more change factors you add, the harder it is to accomplish. We refer to this as the "Seven Degrees of Difficulty" in career change. The seven most common factors are:

1. Location (including international)
2. Function
3. Industry

4. Role (corporate, consultant, small business, solopreneur)
5. Compensation
6. Professional or Management Level
7. Company size

## One Step at a Time

In creating a career plan that includes major changes such as these, we recommend that you focus on one or two factors at a time. It may take longer to work through all the stages, but your odds of success improve dramatically. The easiest job change to make is to do exactly what you are doing now, but in a different setting, hopefully one that helps you move closer to your dream job. For example, if you are in accounting and want to become a hotel manager, the first step might be to get an accounting job in a major hotel chain.

We have one final word of advice. We often hear from clients, "I want to do anything except what I'm doing now." We understand how frustration or unhappiness can get you to this place. However, just doing anything will not necessarily lead you to a *better* place. What employer will hire you to "do anything?"

Moving your career forward is about sensibly putting one foot in front of the other but never losing sight of your ultimate dream job.

# Response to the Cheshire Cat

CONVENTIONAL WISDOM: The most successful people set their career goal early in life and go straight for it. They stay the course and don't detour.

NEW THINKING: Your ultimate career goal may shift with time and experience. The journey could impact your original goal.

*[Alice to Cat] "Would you tell me, please, which way I ought to go from here?"*

*"That depends a good deal on where you want to get to," said the Cat.*

*"I don't much care where—" said Alice.*

*"Then it doesn't matter which way you go," said the Cat.*

*"—so long as I get SOMEWHERE," Alice added as an explanation.*

*"Oh, you're sure to do that," said the Cat, "if you only walk long enough."*

**From Alice in Wonderland**

In our experience, the path to reaching career goals is not always direct. Sometimes, the end goal adjusts to what happens along the way.

Consider this example: A friend wanted to be a brain surgeon when she was in high school. At college she enrolled in the pre-med biology program and she realized brain surgery wasn't going to be right for her. She then serendipitously moved into the school's Forensic Science program and found herself mentored by the department head. During her senior year, another friend sent her an application for an internship at a major city health department's infectious disease laboratory, which she applied for and got. She now heads that lab and has been happily employed there for a number of years. Turns out, she loves that kind of work! Would she have figured that out if she had "stuck to her guns" and refused to veer from her initial goal of becoming a brain surgeon? Probably not.

## Allow Your Destination to Evolve

Not many of us have "perfect" resumes—the right jobs, at the right companies, in the right progression, with the right timing between promotions. More often, we've taken some detours, navigated some roadblocks, and sometimes have even been temporarily lost. Looking back, we often realize our successes can be attributed to these unexpected events. Most of the successful people we know have had careers with plenty of zigs and zags. Of course, along with these comes Monday morning quarterbacking. It's completely normal to look back on your career progression and say to yourself, *"If only I'd been smarter, savvier, or made different decisions, I'd be richer, more famous, and even happier."* We're here to tell you, after working with lots of successful people, don't be too hard on yourself when you deviate from your goals. Sometimes, that very deviation is integral to your success.

As you evolve your career or grow your business, keep in mind that constant evolution prevails. Finding resources, listening to advice, researching information—and the unavoidable time consuming and sometimes expensive "wrong turns"—will take you to the next step and the next. Allow the zigs and zags to shape a successful future.

# Job Search Isn't "Fair"

> **Conventional Wisdom**: Applying, interviewing and getting hired for a job is a logical and fair process.
>
> **New Thinking**: You've got to be in a gaming frame of mind. Finding a job is like playing chess. It's about strategies and moves.

We know a manager who was in charge of a large department that was moving from Chicago to a new facility in Dallas. The move was so time-consuming that the manager hadn't gotten around to hiring his new financial analyst.

Every night he took the resumes home, with plans to look at them before the next day. Of course, that never happened. This went on for a month—maybe longer—until this manager learned that one of the organization's most important vendors was about to cut off the company's line of credit for lack of payment. The situation had to be fixed, and it had to be fixed *now*. The manager trashed the now obsolete resumes and called HR for a fresh batch.

He received 20 more resumes and started at the top of the pile. About three or four resumes in, he found someone who looked like a good prospect. He got an interview scheduled with the candidate for 9 a.m. the next morning, and 48-hours later, this new financial analyst was hired.

Did the new hire do a good job? In fact, he did. But was he the *best* person for the job? Who knows? It's quite possible he wasn't even the best person in the pile. His resume simply happened to be at the right place, in the right time.

Here's another true story. A large national retail company needed to replace a Regional Manager they had just fired. The manager that was being replaced was a woman. To reduce the risk of a lawsuit, the company decided to replace the woman with another woman. So they called the recruiting firm to share their objective. In order to preserve a "perception" of fairness, the company was provided with "a fully diversified slate" of six candidates. Half were women. One was a minority.

The company interviewed all of them. But the point is that the men—no matter how qualified they were or how well they did in the interview—probably didn't have a chance of being hired because the company wanted to hire a woman to mitigate their risk. Did the best person get the job? There's no real way of telling, as that was not the ultimate goal of the search.

We have hundreds of these stories.

## Three Takeaways

What do these stories tell you about the job search process?

1. Job search isn't fair.
2. You will be overlooked for reasons that are not logical, and may even be irrational or biased.
3. Job search isn't fair.

Do you understand how serious we are when we say that "job search isn't fair?"

What can you do about it? You accept that the job search and interview process, such as it is, is broken. Stop looking for the logic in it and buy into the fact that "it is what it is." And steer clear of any advice that assumes you are playing on a level playing field, such as:

- If you have a great resume, you'll get interviews.
- If you write a killer cover letter, you'll grab the hiring manager's attention.
- If you have the right keywords in your resume, it will be chosen by the HR department.
- If you know the right people, you'll get hired.
- If you interview well, you'll get the job.

Job search isn't a game with rules—it's a dance. The job of a recruiter is to find someone to hire, hire them quickly, and not get into trouble with the company or the government while doing it. The recruiter's job is not to hire *you*.

## Networking: The Best Move in the Job Search Dance

Whether internal or external, at least *70% of all successful job searches involve networking*. If your job search strategy is to submit your resume and wait for the phone to ring, or work hard and wait for your boss to notice and promote you, you could be waiting a very long time.

With external job searches, visibility in the market and connecting to others are important. Here are some activities you should consider:

- Attend industry association meetings
- Build a quality LinkedIn profile
- Stay connected to your personal networks

- ▶ Highlight your credibility by giving presentations, writing articles and books, and contributing your knowledge to those in your industry in a meaningful way
- ▶ Research the supply chain for your industry, and determine who you should strategically connect with who might be able to provide you with more job search connections

With internal advancement, self-promotion is important.

- ▶ Realize that hard work won't necessarily translate into a promotion
- ▶ Instead of waiting for them to promote you, sell yourself
- ▶ Understand your organization's culture and politics, and learn how to navigate them
- ▶ Seek out mentors and sponsors
- ▶ Get advice from people who have been successful in the company

Job search is difficult. It can be discouraging and frustrating. And for sure, it is not fair. The job search and interview process is broken, crazy, and not scientific. It's expedient.

So forget fairness, and figure out how to navigate the world as it is. Be opportunistic, be savvy, and engage in the process proactively. Only then will you keep your spirits up and have a good chance of winning.

# Getting Unstuck

CONVENTIONAL WISDOM: If you're stuck in your job search, it's time to get a new resume.

NEW THINKING: If your job search is stalled, it's probably your whole strategy that's not working. (Do you even have a strategy?) And you should be doing a lot more than applying for jobs on the Internet and sending out resumes.

A recent client complained that she had applied to 57 jobs online and sent out 103 resumes so far with absolutely no luck. In most cases, she received no response—not even a simple "thank you for applying" or "we have received your resume." Nothing—unless you count the many recruiting letters for opportunities to sell insurance or multi-level marketing products she received. Her resume was not the issue. She had an excellent resume.

Sound familiar?

If you've been in the job hunt, you may have experienced the same thing to some degree. You have the skill set and experience for the jobs you're applying for. You're pounding the pavement. Your resume is spectacular, but you're just not getting the leads or the interviews you want and deserve. So what could be wrong?

# Three Roadblocks that Impair Your Success

In our experiences, "stuck" job searchers are actually making an effort and investing time and energy. If your job search is going nowhere fast, you have to look deeper into what is impeding your success. Invariably what we discover falls into three buckets:

1.  Lack of a clear focus
2.  Inadequate (or no) strategy
3.  Fear

# Roadblock 1: Lack of Focus

It may seem counterintuitive, but casting a wide net or increasing the circumference of your bull's eye almost never pays off. A focused, well-defined target is far more effective in getting the right doors opened and securing the job leads that could actually produce a job offer. To improve your focus and hone in on your goals, ask yourself the following questions. You may need to do some more soul searching or market research to get good answers.

- ▶ Do you have a crystal clear idea of what your perfect job is?
- ▶ How do you describe your perfect job to others?
- ▶ How well can you articulate your unique attributes that make you a great candidate for your perfect job?
- ▶ Have you identified your target market well enough?
- ▶ What specific companies in your geographic target zone hire people to do what you want to do?
- ▶ How will you trump your competition?

# Roadblock 2: Inadequate Strategy

Maybe your resume does need improvement but more likely you don't have a comprehensive and effective job search strategy to begin with. It seems so logical to sit behind a computer and scan the multitude of Internet job boards such as Indeed.com, Monster.com, or The Ladders. The truth is that even if this approach seems easier 1) it takes a tremendous amount of time to post your information, find relevant jobs, and complete the applications, which are usually very detailed and unique to each job, and 2) it doesn't work. A few people get jobs directly from website postings but not that many do. And most people are disappointed and disillusioned by the process.

The cornerstone of a good job search strategy is networking. You've probably heard that a million times. Maybe you're even tired of hearing it. But have you really *listened*?

In our opinion, networking is so important in job seeking and career advancement that we've devoted an entire section to it in this book. Too many people have lived in a job cocoon, keeping their heads down and focusing on doing a good job, with the flawed assumption that if they do good work, their job will be safe and a successful career will follow. That's just not true anymore. And by failing to develop good networking muscles and a robust contact database, these dedicated, well-intentioned employees can find themselves wandering in the job search wilderness.

# Roadblock 3: Fear

If you're reading this and saying, "But I *have* a well-defined focus and a solid job search strategy, and I'm *still* not getting the leads I want and deserve," you're not alone. Many job seekers are doing these things right, but are still stuck.

If this is you—if your strategy and focus are rock solid but you're still not going anywhere—then something else is going on. What is *really* holding you back?

The pervasive response is "fear." Fear of strangers, fear of embarrassing yourself, fear of failure, fear of rejection, and so on. These powerful, debilitating emotions can stop the most competent and earnest people in their tracks.

Even if it sounds trite, the best advice we can give is to face your fear straight on. Fear can be masquerading as procrastination, Internet job board surfing, and paperwork pushing. If you are stuck in your job search, ask yourself, "What am I afraid of?" And then consider, what is the worst possible outcome if that fear were realized? Most of the time, you can live with the outcome, and often it's really not that bad. If you are still stuck and need an outside, objective perspective, a professional coach can help you identify the core issues and break through the fear that is keeping you from being successful.

# Should I Stay or Should I Go?

In today's "Free Agency" of employment, it's popular to assume that if you are not progressing or being rewarded the way you feel you should, you'll be more successful in a different company. Certainly, more tools are available today to aid in a job search than ever before. In addition, some people feel there are disadvantages to being with a company for "too long."

## Should You Stay?

There are many important benefits of staying with your current company, if that's a reasonable possibility.

1. You already have a network of contacts.
2. You understand the company, its products, and its culture.
3. You have vested benefits, and sometimes these can be worth a lot of money.
4. You have an established reputation and credibility (if you don't, that may be a good reason to leave).

5.  You understand the systems and processes.
6.  You've worked out your personal logistics and lifestyle arrangements.
7.  You may have seniority that matters.

If these factors are worth it to you, then you may want to pursue internal options before you pull the plug on your current company. If you're not happy where you are, or if you feel that you are not being recognized fully, we suggest that you first look at yourself. Are there attitude or performance issues that could be holding you back? If so, do something about them. Second, consider whether another department or job would be a better fit. Finding these opportunities and getting doors opened may require help from your internal network and particularly help from a "sponsor" or mentor.

## Or Should You Go?

There certainly could be good reasons to leave your current company. If you have been involved in a bad, unrecoverable situation, starting over somewhere else may be your best choice. In a different company you can rebuild your reputation from a clean sheet of paper. Another reason to leave is when the pervasive company culture is not a good fit for you. Also, even if you have a good job, the company may be in financial difficulty or you have ethics concerns. (By the way, do not talk about any of these issues in your interviews.) Finally, your company may be in a declining industry, and it's just the right time to leave before all the other mice flee the sinking ship.

# Real-Life Situations

*Henry's Story: A highly qualified Sales Director had taken on a role of re-engineering the outside sales process and installing sophisticated sales tools. Two years later, with the hard part done, the remaining department was in maintenance and upkeep mode. Henry was ready for a new challenge, but no Director positions were open. Furthermore, he was not a good networker. He kept his head down and focused on doing a good job. (How many times have we heard that?!) His first consideration was to find a Sales Director position with another company. He updated his resume, ramped up his networking, and became clearer about what he wanted and what he had to offer. He also revved up his internal networking to see what other options might be available. Fast forward . . . In part because of his dramatically improved visibility inside the company, when a vacancy opened up in a related area a short time later, he was offered a bigger job, bigger department, and a promotion. None of these would have been likely in a reasonable time frame if he had left the company.*

*Sarah's Story: An executive with 20 years of experience and a great track record had been moved to an international role reporting to a boss who did not have a background in her area of expertise. Even though she continued to get strong positive feedback and was achieving every major milestone, she recognized that her boss was never going to be a "sponsor" and would not advocate for her promotion to the next executive level. Even though she could retire with full benefits in nine years, she was ready for more responsibility and wanted to continue her career and professional growth. With her tenure at the company, she would lose a significant amount of money if she left, but under the current organizational structure, she was probably in a dead-end job. She finally concluded that her first course of action would be to aggressively pursue a lateral move back into her functional area of expertise. Then, with a couple more years in a role that was a better fit and with colleagues who would advocate on her behalf, she would assess her advancement options. If, at that time, a promotion was unlikely, she would pursue a position outside the company and negotiate hard in the transition to recover her lost income. She decided if a new job or promotion didn't happen in two years, she would honestly be content doing a bang-up job where she was until she was ready to retire.*

# Your Four Choices

At the end of the day, if you are unhappy with your job, you have these options:

1. Make personal adjustments in your current job that earn the recognition and rewards you desire.
2. Pursue other opportunities in the same company that are a better fit.
3. Seek a suitable position outside the company; or
4. Reconcile yourself to your current situation (hopefully with a good attitude).

We think this is the right order of priority for long-term success.

# How Broad Is Too Broad?

---

CONVENTIONAL WISDOM: The broader your definition of the job that you want, the better your opportunity to get a job.

NEW THINKING: If your definition is too broad, you are not really an attractive candidate for anything to anyone.

---

Too often when asked, "What kind of job are you looking for?" people say, "I have lots of skills and experience. I can do several things." The thinking is that it's better to be flexible and open rather than miss an opportunity. However, we find that if you're not more precise about what kind of job you want, you may not get a job at all. For example, when people say things like, "I'm looking for a job where I can use my problem solving and great communication skills," or if they are all over the map, then their friends and associates won't know how to help them.

Which statement is more helpful in a networking situation?
- **A.** I'm looking for a challenging position that allows me to use my diverse experience and skills.
- **B.** I'm looking for a HR management position where my recruiting and training skills will benefit a company's fast growing demand for top talent.

Many people will think "A" is the safer way to go. Often job seekers are so concerned about missing out on chances for a job that they create generic descriptions that could fit nearly any position. They're reluctant to be industry specific and worry that narrowing their target to a specific job or role will cut off other opportunities.

## The Name of the Game Is Balance

You probably don't want to restrict your prospects by being too specific—naming exactly what you want to do, down to job titles and company name—but you also want to avoid being so vague that the recruiter or hiring manager has no clue what job you're applying for. Your goal should be to strike a balance between the two. If you're unsure how precise or narrow to be, we find that more people go too broad rather than too narrow.

How do you strike a good balance?

First, we suggest that you go "job shopping" on the Internet. Try to find job postings that match exactly what you're looking for, no matter where they are located. These position descriptions give you the road map for what experience, education, and personal characteristics employers are looking for. Working from these "sample" postings, you can develop your resume, online profile, and networking introduction to be in alignment with the key ingredients.

Be as precise as possible without getting too carried away. A sharp focus is your friend, not your enemy. It's unlikely that you're looking for the one job out of only three that exist in the Universe. Once you've researched and cultivated a target list of companies and contacts that you can leverage in your networking efforts, it may represent only 10% of your original list. The good news is that the 10% you're focusing on will be a far better fit for your profile. In turn, you will be significantly more successful in generating interest, getting introductions, and landing a job.

Remember, if you're willing to settle for just any old job, you might get any old job. And in no time, you could be right back in job search mode again.

# "Career Plan" — Oxymoron?

**CONVENTIONAL WISDOM:** Careers are the outcomes of a series of jobs.

**NEW THINKING:** The most successful careers come from intention, planning, and lifetime career management.

Are you someone who has carefully planned most steps in your career? If so, you're one of the few. Most people would admit that they don't have—and have never had—a career plan. In fact, most careers are products of "happenstance," not planning. Thus, "career plan" is actually an *oxymoron*. Sad. But true.

> **ox·y·mo·ron** (äk-sE-›mor-»än) **n.** a combination of contradictory or incongruous words (as *sweet sorrow*); something (as a concept) that is made up of contradictory or incongruous elements.

How does this happen? For most of us, it starts with a specific course of study (resulting in an undergraduate degree or technical qualification) that is frequently chosen because of various outside factors: parents, counselors, cost, logistics, and more. Many of us end up in areas unrelated to our true passions. We can spend twenty years or more in unsatisfying jobs just to discover at mid-career that a major change is necessary.

Most executives admit that their careers have evolved based on opportunism, hard work, and sometimes luck. The truth is that many savvy executives manage their business goals far better than they manage their careers, leaving them sometimes displaced or dissatisfied with their ultimate achievements. Of course, at this stage, a dramatic career shift can be difficult, not to mention expensive. And scary.

What can be done about it? Two things:

1. Start very early in your career with a career plan.
2. Create a career plan right now, and get on with it.

## Career Plans

You wouldn't operate a business without a business plan, nor should you embark upon a career or continue down the path you're traveling without a plan in place. Successful businesses have plans—strategic and tactical. Effective action follows the creation of a meaningful plan. Significant insight and discovery about the business is, in fact, derived from the planning process itself. A career planning process can deliver the same kind of insight and discovery. Because there are so many options and avenues to consider, having a plan will allow you to focus time and energy productively on achieving maximum career satisfaction and success.

Creating a good career plan is simple but not easy. You should start with the end in mind—a vision—but that is not always obvious.

## Steps to Get Started

First, clarify "who you are." *You* are the raw material you have to work with. What are your special gifts and unique talents? Inventory your skills and capabilities. Focus on what you are good at, and don't spend too much time "developing" your weaknesses. Also, understand your particular personality traits and styles. There are a variety of excellent assessment instruments that can be used to gain a useful view of yourself. Two popular instruments that have withstood the test of time are Campbell Interests and Skills Survey (CISS) found at profiler.com and Motivational Appraisal for Personal Potential (MAPP) found at assessment.com.

Once you have a fix on who you are, explore what you really love. What are you passionate about? What subjects capture your imagination and grab your attention on a regular basis? Once you have uncovered your true passions in life, there are lots of ways to do what you love. Here are some ideas.

- ▶ Do it.
- ▶ Work for a company that does it.
- ▶ Provide a service related to it.
- ▶ Teach it.
- ▶ Write about it.
- ▶ Speak about it.
- ▶ Create a product related to it.
- ▶ Sell or broker it.
- ▶ Promote it.
- ▶ Organize it.
- ▶ Set up, repair, restore, fix, or maintain it.

Next, create your vision. What do you want to be doing in five to ten years? Get out of your own way. Suspend your doubt. Think big. Create your dream job. Write down your important goals. Where will you be? What kind of company or people will you be working with? What level of management do you aspire to? How will you spend most of your time?

Once your vision is defined, compare it to where you are now, and list the gaps. For each gap, compile the steps to close it. What is the most logical thing to do next? Choose a few goals that can be accomplished first, and so on. A career plan will emerge. Give yourself targets and dates. Be realistic about the time and money required.

# Get Started and Get Unstuck

Taking that first step in your plan is the most critical. Every baby step forward is a giant step toward your ultimate career and personal contentment.

Consider finding a career coach to help you through the process and to encourage you through the transition. Investments in training and support pay off in thousands of ways.

# The Grass Is Not Always Greener

---

**CONVENTIONAL WISDOM**: Corporate executives can easily become consultants, and successful consultants can become corporate leaders.

**NEW THINKING**: Less than 20% are good cross-over candidates.

---

Every time the economy expands or dips, executives who are tired, bored, displaced, or in search of above-market earnings come out of the barn in droves looking for "greener pastures." They frequently assume that their experiences running a "real" company qualify them to provide insight and expertise as a consultant to other companies or executives.

Meanwhile, consultants looking for financial stability have thoughts of going corporate. Consultants are often confident of their abilities to lead organizations. Who could be better qualified than them to run a company from the inside? After all, they have been the guiding hand for many companies' strategic, financial, and technology directions. They have been trusted counsel for their top executives.

Unfortunately, grazing in the other "greener" pasture is more complicated that it seems on the surface.

# What Life Is Like as a Consultant

The defining characteristics of the consulting environment are remarkably similar from firm to firm, regardless of whether it is a large global firm or a small local firm. First and foremost, at a senior level, success is based on the generation of sales revenue. Dollars equal power.

As a consultant, engagements are driven by thought leadership and strategy. Your clients typically have a list of problems that need to be solved—and the list changes frequently. Corporate decision-makers ensure that consultants have special access to people and resources. After all, they have already, or will shortly, write a very large check for their services.

From a delivery perspective, work is often standardized and methodology-based. Engagements have a beginning, an end, and a defined scope. Often little or no responsibility for implementation or outcomes is specified.

But, there are some exceptions. Certain contractual arrangements have shared responsibility for results, and that is reflected in the fee. Secondly, consultants handle implementation of systems or processes. However, once it is done, consultants still leave and don't have to live with the consequences. Supervision and personnel responsibility is usually limited to performance on the projects by the team members.

# Should You Be a Consultant?

- ▸ Do you enjoy a continuously shifting landscape of new problems to solve?
- ▸ Is selling fun? Do you like the thrill of the chase?
- ▸ Do you enjoy socializing and building a network of contacts?
- ▸ Are you energized by smart people doing interesting work?
- ▸ Are you easily bored?

▶ Do you like providing "advice and counsel" with little responsibility for operational activities or outcomes?

## What Life Is Like as a Corporate Executive

In corporations, whether public or private, profitability and shareholder value are the focus. For most executives, success is based on contribution to operating results.

Organizational leadership drives performance, from vision to planning through execution. Decision-making and risk taking, with accountability for choices, are fundamental. Outcomes are everything. Activities are heavily implementation and results driven. Typically projects are not intellectually stimulating.

Most of the work of the organization is continuous and predominantly operational. Much is policy and procedurally based. There is a broad distribution of people in a corporation, with a tendency to gather around the mean in intelligence, motivation, and interest in their work. Comprehensive personnel management is required by line and most staff executives to maximize the contribution of all employees in the company.

## Should You Become a Corporate Executive?

▶ Do you like being on the front lines, directing others, making choices?

▶ Do you like to see things through to the end?

▶ Do you gain personal satisfaction from positive, measurable results that you had a significant role in delivering?

▶ Can you keep focus on the long-term while dealing with tactical and operational concerns?

▶ Are you willing to stand behind your decisions and be accountable for outcomes with continuing consequences?

▶ As an insider, can you gain the respect of others for your business acumen?

- ▸ Are you energized by motivating and leading groups of people to successful achievement of common goals?
- ▸ Do others follow you and support you?

## Aligning Yourself with the Choice You Make

If you are a *consultant* and still think you are a candidate for a change to a corporation, consider whether you are most suited for a consulting-like role or for an operating leadership position. Your business acumen, facilitation ability, and communication skills are key skills that will be valuable in a corporate role.

If you are an *executive* and still want to try your hand at consulting, consider whether you are most suited for a partner (translate that to sales) role or for delivery management (translate that to project or multiple projects). Your experience of making things work in the real world and your ability to navigate complex organizations will be helpful in a consulting role.

Both consulting and executive roles have challenges and rewards. Neither is as easy as it seems from the outside, looking in. As long as you find the one that works for you, you will be where the grass is greenest.

# Is It Your Business or Your Hobby?

CONVENTIONAL WISDOM: Print some business cards and you're in business.

NEW THINKING: Your commitment to being in business is reflected in everything you do.

As small business owners, we frequently seek other small businesses to provide services. We also have coached clients and colleagues about starting and running small businesses. As for our vendors, we have some we would not trade for anything. We work directly with the principals who have special talents, whose counsel is always on the mark, and who have been instrumental in the success of our businesses. They have done exactly what we need them to do at a price we can afford.

But contacting some of them? Well, that's another matter. They use their cell phones as their primary business phones, have not bothered to record appropriate messages, and often do not return calls (or emails)—even after multiple messages. What does it say about their businesses when a computer voice says, "You have reached 555-123-4567?"

Similarly, some small business vendors do not take credit cards. Credit cards provide more control over cash flow, financial reporting, convenience, safety, and even loyalty points, all of which are especially important to their small business customers.

Many former executives or business professionals leave Corporate America to go into business for themselves. Too often they are clueless when it comes to setting up even the most rudimentary infrastructure for a market presence, client management, technology, accounting, and communication—and have done little to figure it out.

Ultimately, customers may tolerate these things if they are getting critical products or services they don't think they could get easily find elsewhere. But it can be frustrating to do business with these companies.

## If You Want to Be in Business, Then Act Like It

The common denominator here is whether these people really want to be "in business." When pressed, some of them are "in hobby" and others are "in denial." In either case, they are not fully motivated to put in the time or the effort to be credible and really successful.

If this resonates with you, consider if you want to be in business for real. If you do, be sure to create a solid foundation for the business—at least the basics. Here's a short 10-point checklist:

1. *Company name:* Choose it with your email and website domain availability in mind.

2. *Domain:* Once you have your company name, lock in your domain and maybe several derivatives.

3. *Email:* In the beginning, you can start with your company name at Yahoo or Gmail—eventually you will probably want to use your company domain and host your account.

4. *Website:* Create a simple one using one of the many templates available. To start, you only need a few basic pages—Home, Your Bio, Your Services, and Contact Information. A starter website is informational, so you can send people there. Getting your website to show up in the search engines is much more complicated and expensive.

5. *Communication:* Cell phones are fine, as long as you treat your cell phone as an "office" phone with an appropriate message. Be sure to check it often and respond professionally. Same goes for email.

6. *Company Structure:* Sole proprietorship, LLC or Incorporated/Sub-Chapter S—your choice here will determine what else you need to do. Get an expert accountant or lawyer to advise you.

7. *Company Bank Account:* You will want to set up a separate company checking account and credit card, and make arrangements to accept credit cards.

8. *Accounting System:* You need to invoice customers, record payments, make payments for purchases, and track expenses for financial and tax purposes. This can be done "manually" (e.g. using MS Word and Excel), or you can use a small business accounting system like QuickBooks.

9. *Technology:* Consider what you need and if you will need help supporting it. How long can you be without your computer or other technology and still serve your customers? What can be done with mobile devices, and what requires more robust equipment?

10. *Cost:* There is an up-front and on-going cost to running a business. Do you have the resources for a basic business set up and continuing operations?

This gets you set up. Now, of course, you will need to address your products/services, your target customers and how to sell to them, and your financial objectives and resources.

Just because you're a small business doesn't mean you can't make a big impact. The first step is acting like you're in business. Be professional—your customers will notice and appreciate it.

# "Jack-of-All-Trades" Is *Not* a Job Title

CONVENTIONAL WISDOM: Companies are looking for problems solvers, utility players, and creative thinkers.

NEW THINKING: Personal characteristics are important, but they only matter in the context of the job requirements.

Any time we're tasked with helping a client with a resume, one of the first questions we ask is, "What kind of work do you do?"

Many times—in fact, too many times—the answer is something along the lines of . . .

"Well, I've done a lot of things," "I have lots of transferable skills," "I've had an eclectic career," and one of the most popular, "I'm a Jack-of-all-Trades." We even had one executive tell us she was a "utility player." Somewhere along the way, she had read that companies were looking for utility players.

When someone gives us an answer like this, we try to delve a little deeper by asking the question, "What kind of job are you looking for?" Sometimes we get a meaty answer that will give us something to build on. Other times we get answers like, "I'm willing to do anything," or "There are lots of things that I could do."

# Flexibility Is Nice, But Function Is Key

Flexibility is a valuable attribute. Who doesn't enjoy working with flexible colleagues and co-workers? And it's certainly true that companies are looking for people who are adaptable and willing to do what the company needs.

Remember that while your willingness to be a flexible team player might be a tiebreaker, it's not the main thing that employers are looking for. An organization looking to hire a sales manager wants candidates with certain skills, experience, education, and knowledge, just as a company hiring an accountant is looking for a set of different—yet still specific—capabilities. Companies hire people to perform certain functions and need to be convinced of a candidate's value-added contribution in performing those specific responsibilities. For a moment, put yourself in the hiring manager's shoes. How would you react if a candidate said, "I can do lots of things. What job do you have for me?"

# Characteristics Are Not Job Titles

Simply put, "Jack-of-All-Trades" doesn't appear on any organization chart—with the possible exception of specially created jobs for existing employees to fill a specific need—and they still don't call it "Jack-of-All-Trades."

If you have fallen into this trap yourself or others have extolled the virtues of your diverse skill set, we invite you to reconsider. What is the *job* that you can credibly convince a hiring manager you can do and bring value to the role? Be specific about your relevant talents, skills, experience, and knowledge. Once you've defined yourself in terms of a real job, and not by characteristics, you will need to frame your personal presentation and resume to support your claims.

# Business Roller Coasters: Are We Having Fun Yet?

CONVENTIONAL WISDOM: Change is discreet. It is an event to work through.

NEW THINKING: Change is continuous. It is the normal condition of things.

When "change management" became popular in the early 90s, a handy little book called *Business as Unusual* by Price Pritchett became *de rigueur* reading for any managers worth their salt. It was filled with clever, short essays about what a manager needed to know as an organization went through some sort of major change or upheaval. Some of the helpful little tidbits included "Re-recruit good people" and "Take care of the 'me' issues in a hurry."

Ah, how times have changed. While these axioms are probably still relevant, the notion that change is "an event" is outdated. Today, change just *is*. In order to effectively manage change, we first have to expect change and be prepared for it. It's "business as usual." The one and only certainty is that tomorrow will not be like today. Technology is advancing at lightning speed, business models are evolving more rapidly than ever, and competitive markets are increasingly attracted to the next shiny thing.

# The Only Constant Is Change

The most powerful and effective success strategies demand flexibility. Consider your future and your overall state of mind if you knew you were sufficiently adaptable and energized to tackle any unexpected development in your job or your organization. Then, ask yourself the following three questions:

1. What would I do differently?
2. What new skills would I need?
3. How would this confidence affect my performance today?

# Adaptability Equals Success

Consider today's most successful companies. What do you notice about them? Among the many things these companies excel at is building cultures that embrace innovation, adaptability, and flexibility. They've introduced and kept up with new technology, have consistently introduced new product lines, and aren't afraid to enter new markets. They often have a parade of new, innovative products and services. Long lines of customers tell you all you need to know.

# Are You Up to the Challenge?

Spend some time thinking about and developing a plan to react to the following questions.

- How can I be an agent of change in my specific job or area?
- What will I do to help the company move the needle "up, up and away," toward a possibly chaotic but exhilarating future?
- What's it going to take for me to enjoy the ride?

And when the ride starts to get a little bumpy—and it will, no matter how much fun you're having—when you start to feel as if you've had enough change, or are doubting the positive nature of change, remember what Charles Darwin said, "It's not the strongest species that survive, not the most intelligent, but the most responsive to change."

# Workforce Orbiting and Reentry

CONVENTIONAL WISDOM: You can go back to work after a few years and pick up where you left off.

NEW THINKING: Workforce reentry is problematic and requires a targeted strategy.

*And I think it's gonna be a long, long time*
*Till touchdown brings me round again to find*
*I'm not the man [or woman] they think I am at home*
*Oh no, no, no, I'm a rocket man.*

**Lyrics from "Rocket Man" by Elton John**

Wouldn't it be nice if we could jump into a career time machine and just step into the career flow where we left off a few (or many) years ago? We are huge advocates of those parental words of wisdom, "Whatever you want to do, if you want it bad enough and your put your mind to it, you can do it." We're also the first people to encourage anyone to put their mind and grit into whatever their career or job goals are and just go do it.

Here's the truth. If you have been out of the job market for a while, it's extremely difficult, if not downright impossible, to reenter exactly where you left off. Things have changed. And the longer you were out, the more exponential the challenge. We commonly see women (and some men) who have put their careers on hold to care for children, aging parents, or both. This is exacerbated when the displaced homemaker is forced back to work because of a divorce, loss of a spouse, or economic demands. Other professionals take intentional career detours, sometimes into business for themselves or independent consulting, and they discover it doesn't work well for them or they lose their shirt. We also see older individuals who "retired early," but whose retirement funds have been severely depleted—from financial losses or illness for example—and they need income to recover their financial security.

## First, the Bad News

If you are in the last five years of your career, finding full-time employment in your dream job may be unrealistic. There are certainly exceptions for people who are uniquely qualified for jobs that are hard to fill. But for the vast majority of jobs, a company is more likely to hire and invest in a younger candidate who they believe has a longer "shelf life." It's simple economics. Plus companies are reluctant to put an end-of-career professional into a job that could be a career track stepping stone for younger, high potential employees.

Hopefully, you look ten years younger than you are and have no physical manifestations or symptoms of being a "senior citizen." If so, go for it. Theoretically employers are not supposed to ask your age, so you might fly under the radar and get the job. Beware the tricky questions though, and don't innocently volunteer information that will give your age away. They might ask you what year you graduated from school/college. You might even have that on your resume. Don't start talking about your grandchildren or your retirement plans. You'd be surprised how many people naively blurt out these things. Assuming you are young looking and vibrant, you will still have some hurdles to overcome.

If you look your age or even approximately so, you may have to seriously consider a contract job, part-time work, freelance gigs, or consulting. Contracts can pay nicely and provide an excellent source of steady income. There are numerous staffing agencies that place contract workers, some of whom are offered full-time employment. It's sort of a "try and buy" recruitment model for companies. Further, according to the American Staffing Association, some 79% of temporary employees actually work full-time. Contracts can be for several months and even a year or more. Plus, many agencies provide career counseling and free training. Ultimately, it's their business to find competent talent and place these individuals into contract positions for their clients.

More experienced professionals and senior executives with specific content or industry expertise should consider consulting. Being self-employed has some valuable benefits.

- ▶ You set your own schedule.
- ▶ You charge whatever the market will bear.
- ▶ You get to do exactly what you know (and presumably love).
- ▶ You really don't have a "boss" to answer to, other than your clients.

Of course, there are a few downsides to being self-employed as well.

- ▶ You must be good at selling yourself and your expertise.
- ▶ You must be willing and able to manage the volatility of your finances, and realistically should have a three- to six-month liquidity safety net at all times.

A lot of smart, talented people are not good at selling themselves. And gifted sales people are rare. The rest of us are programmed not to brag about ourselves and not to be too pushy. In a professionally appropriate way, that's what a consultant has to do— talk about what they know and how they can benefit the company, and be persistent and thorough in following up on sales leads. While these may not be in your DNA, they can be learned. With the right tools, skills, determination, and mindset, smart, experienced people can crack the code on consulting success.

The final bit of bad news is that while you've been gone, technology and the sheer volume of knowledge have continued to advance at a shocking pace. Thus, no matter what industry or job you hail from, it is a virtual certainty that the technology you were using "way back when" is gone and replaced by something radically different. The knowledge base you mastered when you were last employed may have doubled or quadrupled.

## Now, the Good News

There are a few crucial keys to workforce reentry you must master. And if you do, you will increase the odds of finding a suitable reentry point that will be both enjoyable and rewarding.

> ▶ *First, get your mojo going.* "When you're away for a few years you may feel you don't have much to offer or you may feel less confident," said Marcia Brumit Kropf, Vice President of Research and Information Services for Catalyst, a New York-based research organization. Getting back into the flow of things may seem daunting, but whatever you need to do to cultivate your optimism and confidence is job one. Work with a coach or career counselor right at the start. They can help you inventory your skills and interests and evaluate your best options. Plus, they can be your sounding board and cheerleader throughout the reentry process, helping you to stay on course and keep a positive attitude. If you can't afford a professional coach, look for one who will barter with you. Surely you have something you can trade. If that doesn't work, there are not-for-profit organizations that provide career services and job search support.

▶ *Have a "bulls-eye" job in mind.* The best way you can recruit your friends, family, and colleagues to help you is to give them specific ways to help. If you just tell them, "I'm going back to work and could use your help," what are they supposed to do with that information? You have to do your research. First, assess what you are interested in doing, what you're skilled to do, and what you will be considered a good candidate for. You might have to take a lower level job to make up for lost time and position yourself to be competitive. Then, look for companies and organizations in your targeted geographic area that offer these jobs. It doesn't matter if they don't have the kind of job you want posted on their website or on the Internet. What you really want is to get out there and start networking. When your friends ask how they can help you, you can specifically tell them, "I'm looking for introductions into… [the target list of companies you created]." And you can tell them exactly the kind of job you would be interested in and qualified for. Who knows, they just may have a lead.

▶ *Refresh your knowledge of technology and recent developments in your field.* Technology and information may have advanced radically since you were last employed. If you really want to be considered an attractive job candidate, you have to race up that learning curve with gusto. Take a class or classes. You can't afford to be obsolete before you start. And there's a good chance you won't get hired if the employer concludes that you are too far out of date to invest in your training. You also need to know the "language" that's current in your field. Every industry creates its own new buzz words and phrases, and you need to be in the know to pull off a good interview. Many colleges and universities, especially community colleges, offer excellent and affordable continuing adult education courses that can help you brush up your skills and learn new applications. You may even qualify for free re-training through your state's workforce commission. Some of these courses are offered through distance learning, allowing you to take the class at home and at your own pace. If you can't take a class, then at least go to the library and catch up, or just ask your friends and colleagues to conduct tutorials for you. Don't be afraid or embarrassed to ask. Most people really do want to help.

▶ ***Learn how to network and dedicate yourself to it.*** We probably beat this drum more often than any other with our career transition clients. You are most likely to find your job through somebody you know or somebody they know. You are not likely to find your next job on the Internet job boards. At the very most—and some say this number is too high—only about 15-20 percent of all available jobs are publicly advertised in any medium, and only about 5 percent of job-seekers obtain jobs directly through ads of any kind—print and Internet. What people often don't realize is how inefficient these job boards are. Please don't be one of those people who spend the majority of their job search time shopping the Internet for the needle in the haystack. Even if you find it, the odds that your application or resume will be "the one" is miniscule.

Networking, on the other hand, is the key—for any job at any level. Just consider that for years we have heard about the "six degrees of separation." Now, according to research conducted by the University of Milan and scientists at Facebook, here in the United States we are just over *four* degrees of separation. So when you are coming back into the workplace, what better place to start than with former colleagues, classmates, friends, and yes, even your family. These are people who know you, know about you, and are more likely to give you some latitude than a stranger. Ask questions, ask for recommendations, and ask for introductions.

▶ ***Brush up on your interviewing.*** Here's another area where working with a coach or career adviser can add value to your search. In particular, they can help you craft a resume that maximizes your value and skills and minimizes your "time off." Even with a well-honed resume, you still have to answer the tough interview questions, like "What have you been doing since your last job?" You have to tell the truth. Hopefully you have not been sitting in a recliner watching TV or playing video games the whole time. Chances are you have been doing something productive and building some new skills along the way. When you look closely at your activities and skills through this lens, you can share with confidence what you've invested your time in, and what you've learned as a result. No apologies. Candor and creativity pay off here. With a positive attitude, a command of current developments and technology, and a polished presentation, hiring managers should be able to look past a gap in your work experience.

## Looking Ahead

If you choose to take some time off in the future or you end up out of the workforce for an extended period of time, here are two things to pay attention to right from the beginning.

1.  Stay current. Keep your skills sharp. Stay up to date on new technologies and developments in your field. Stay involved in your professional associations— it's a great environment to network at the same time that you are keeping abreast of new information.

2.  Do something that matters to your future employment. Imagine a time in the future when you want to go back to work. What will you put on your resume then? Take classes, cultivate new skills, write articles, learn a new language, do a few freelance gigs, get involved in volunteer activities that a future employer might value, maintain any pertinent certifications, and get new ones.

## Job Search Flow Chart

**Focus**
- Figure out what you want to do and where you want to work.
- Carefully define your next job, incorporating what you will be considered a good candidate.

**Prepare**
- Develop your marketing materials (resume, bio, cover letter) to be in alignment with your desired next job.
- Create or update your LinkedIn profile to reflect your new resume.
- Start building your LinkedIn network; aggressively add connections from your current/prior jobs, industry and community activities, social sphere, and even family.

**Aim**
- Research what companies have those jobs in your desired geographic area.
- Create a Target List of companies you want to work for.
- Identify key people in those companies with whom you want to connect.

**Network**
- Ask for introductions to your target list of people and companies.
- Check company websites and job boards for positions that might interest you.

**Interview**
- Prepare thoroughly for each interview.
- Take interviews for practice.
- Follow up religiously.

**Negotiate**
- Evaluate all economic facets of the offer.
- Counter-offer to ask for more money or other benefits (e.g. title, vacation time)
- Keep selling all the way to the end.

**Work**
- Priority one—get to know all the key people around you.
- Deliver exceptional performance—ask questions if you don't know something.
- Continue to network—never stop.

# Assessments vs. Truth

**CONVENTIONAL WISDOM:** Good career counseling starts with an assessment.

**NEW THINKING:** Assessments can be useful and thought provoking, but they are not the linchpin for meaningful career discussions.

*Before one studies Zen, mountains are mountains and waters are waters.*
*After a first glimpse into the truth of Zen, mountains are no longer mountains*
*and waters are no longer waters.*
*After enlightenment, mountains are once again mountains and waters are once*
*again waters.*

**Zen saying**

How are job-related skills and abilities usually measured in professional development and career planning? These days, there are hundreds of assessments that measure a plethora of personality traits, preferences, styles, and strengths and they vary widely in terms of sophistication and credibility. Some career counselors even mandate starting with one or more. There are three major types used to differentiate people.

▶ **Personality assessments** are used to assess characteristics that affect behaviors in personal and social relationships.

▶ **Cognitive ability or achievement assessments** are used to assess verbal, nonverbal, and psychomotor abilities, intelligence, or mastery of knowledge in a particular content area.

▶ **Interest and aptitude assessments** are used to assess likes, dislikes, and patterns of interest that may relate to specific occupations. These are commonly used in career counseling.

# All They're Cracked Up to Be?

Certainly, assessments can provide meaningful insights as part of the career planning process. All too frequently, however, we see them misused and misunderstood. Here are a few cautions.

▶ **Quality.** The quality of these instruments varies widely. A legitimate assessment measures what it says it does, and the results are repeatable and yield consistent scores under consistent conditions. Some popular assessments are notoriously unreliable and may not have sufficient research or testing to back up their claims. Just making it to the *New York Times* bestseller list does not ensure that the assessment is valid. These "bad" assessments are often embraced by people who do not have a full understanding of the product, its foundation, and its proper application.

▶ **Usage**. Career counselors, advisers, and coaches are increasingly being encouraged to use assessments as a foundation for counseling and coaching because they provide a vehicle for starting the client conversation. This seems like a cop out. What would they do if they didn't have an assessment to prime the pump? Sadly, the way assessments are marketed, they often provide a significant revenue source for the consultant and a strong financial incentive to use them just to make more money.

▶ **Credentials**. Assuming a particular assessment is credible, too often the person administering the assessment is not qualified to understand and communicate the results. The more sophisticated instruments are available only through certified consultants. Hopefully their credentials provide at least a minimal level of confidence. However, more and more assessments can be purchased retail and taken online. Some assessments allow results to be immediately downloaded upon completion. A trained, qualified professional can help the purchaser translate and apply the information from the report to their particular situation. On the other hand, because they are readily available, some professionals offer them without having received adequate training. Or, you can bypass the professional altogether and just read the report yourself. However, just reading a printed report spit out by the computer may not deliver an accurate or thorough enough interpretation of the data.

# You Are More Than Your Results

It's so tempting to fall into the trap of thinking that assessment results represent a form of "truth." In fact, no matter how good an assessment is, it's a snapshot in time of a specific set of attributes being measured specifically by that instrument. It is not a representation of your whole identity. It's not a measure of your skills. It's not a measure of your values, beliefs, or "goodness" as a person. There is an entire universe of information and characteristics that any assessment does not—and cannot—measure.

We often notice that when a candidate receives a particularly interesting and presumably relevant assessment, an epiphany occurs. They start filtering the rest of the world into these "categories" or characteristics. They even internalize the results into their brand and identity and put signs on their office doors or desk declaring, "I am an ENFJ," "I am a Yellow," "I am a Researcher." No, you're more than that. Much more than that. It's just not that simple, and yet this new discovery of "truth" can be contagious and pervasive.

Ultimately, when you expand your experience with assessments, over time you will build a collage that more accurately and perceptibly portrays who you are. With many different ways of understanding what makes you tick, you will probably come back to earth and lose your missionary zeal for the assessment of the month.

For now, if you are the job seeker or career counseling client, we encourage you to verify the credentials and qualifications of the counselor or consultant, and check out the credibility of the instruments that are being recommended. Depending on cost and your level of clarity about your goals, assessments can be quite valuable, but it's not the only way to get to a good result.

# Parting Is Such Sweet Sorrow
## ... or Is It?

CONVENTIONAL WISDOM: Keep your ear to the ground and watch for signs of trouble, in the company or in your situation, so that you can get ahead of the curve. Take charge of making a job change before the company does it for you.

NEW THINKING: Take charge of your career, not just one job. Having a well-prepared, viable exit strategy for continuous growth is a powerful tool in your long-term career management arsenal.

*You got to know when to hold 'em, know when to fold 'em,*
*Know when to walk away and know when to run.*

**Lyrics from "The Gambler" by Kenny Rogers**

You should know by now that your career is in your own hands. As a "free agent" you have to learn how to effectively represent yourself throughout your career—in, out, up, down, and sideways. While we all know people who have, for very good reasons, stayed at the same company for 20 years, these days that type of longevity is more likely to be viewed as a negative than a positive by recruiters and hiring managers.

The three important messages we have about leaving a job or company are these:

1.  Planning ahead in terms of when and how you will leave is more essential than ever.
2.  When it comes to leaving, there are guidelines that will increase your chances of success.
3.  Don't burn bridges.

## Exiting as a Career Strategy

Today, developing a strategy for leaving a job is almost as important as developing a strategy for finding one. Companies simply don't guarantee lifetime employment anymore. A couple of decades ago employees could count on being employed by Papa Company from "cradle to grave." Those days are long gone. In today's fiercely competitive global economy more organizations than ever are downsizing, right-sizing, reorganizing, outsourcing, off-shoring, and merging in order to stay alive. In this atmosphere no one's job is safe.

In addition, companies are often less involved in career planning, promotional tracking, and directing employees' advancement. Individuals must take responsibility for their own growth and career success. What that means, then, is that no matter what job you're in or aspirations you hold, it is crucial for you to always, and we do mean *always*, have an exit strategy planned.

There are a few specific situations in which an employee should have a defined, intentional exit strategy.

▶ **Newly hired college graduates who want to return to school for an advanced degree down the road**. Most top-notch business graduate schools prefer candidates who have worked for at least a couple of years. To that end, if you take a job right after receiving your undergraduate degree and know for sure that you want to get your MBA or equivalent, you really should have a specific strategy in mind sooner rather than later. Many companies offer generous tuition reimbursement programs when you're ready to go back to school. Working out your exit or transition plan ahead of time may allow you to capitalize on your company's support and post-degree opportunities. Handled properly, you can also retain the goodwill of your employer if you depart.

▶ **Someone who has agreed to take a "development job" in order to learn or improve valuable new skills, but the job does not fit their natural talents or professional "sweet spot."** These can be important career growth opportunities, but the danger is getting stuck in a job where you are never going to be great. Your stress level will probably be higher, your performance reviews could suffer, and the potential growth opportunity could, in fact, derail your otherwise stellar track record. In these situations, we recommend you negotiate terms and conditions, specifically how and when you will transition out, before you take the gig.

▶ **A working environment or boss that is just plain toxic.** This happens far too often in companies with cutthroat cultures, unenlightened leadership, or an obsession with short-term performance. Sometimes, you just have to get out. If your working environment or boss is taking a serious toll on your morale, satisfaction, or health ... RUN! However, be smart about it and don't burn any bridges. In most cases you'll be more successful in your transition if you don't pull the rip cord right away in anger or panic. Instead, find a way to handle the immediate stressors so you can bide your time while you put together a viable, realistic, and achievable exit strategy. You may find opportunities in other parts of the same company where you can escape the poison of your current situation. Or, you may have to leave the company altogether. Find a career coach or an independent adviser to help you figure it out.

# Tips for Exit-Ready Career Management

Leaving your job, your company, or even your department or position is normal these days. In fact, it's pervasive. We've compiled a few tips we think are important when exiting, but typically aren't emphasized or executed well. Way too many of our clients have ignored, been naïve about, or fallen short of handling these simple elements.

▸ Have a current resume—update it every year.

▸ Keep track of your accomplishments so you can include them accurately on your resume and talk about them in interviews.

▸ Build your network and keep it fresh. The best time to build it? When you don't need it. It doesn't matter how long ago you knew the person or in what context. If they're still alive, they're a networking contact.

▸ Dedicate yourself to expanding your skills and credentials.

▸ Constantly scan the horizon for what's happening in the industry, the community, and the field.

▸ Keep all your critical documents, such as recommendation letters, awards, certificates, diplomas, articles, and media coverage, in one place. A handy 3-ring binder works well as a career portfolio. Or, scan the important paper documents and save them electronically in a career portfolio folder.

Jobs, companies, and whole industries are fluid these days. The best strategies for companies and for careers require adaptability—there is no way to predict the game-changing events that can immerge in an instant. So having a career plan in place that includes a variety of pathways to achieve your ultimate goals will give you peace of mind and self-confidence to handle any curve ball that gets thrown your way.

# Resignations: More than Legal

CONVENTIONAL WISDOM: Once you give notice, you're mostly free to do or say what you want.

NEW THINKING: How you handle yourself as you depart is just as important as when you start.

Whether you've got a new job or have decided to quit without one, yes, how you resign matters—and may even affect you for the rest of your career. Many people fail to recognize the importance of the explicit and implicit messages they send when they resign. This is the time to build—not burn—bridges. What you communicate will be remembered. No matter what your experience on the job has been, now is the time to create a positive picture of your experience and the value of your relationships.

## First Things First—Put It in Writing

It is advantageous to resign with a letter that formally documents the decision. Not only is this considerate, it also protects you. It creates legal documentation of when you left, that you gave appropriate notice, and that you left voluntarily. The letter should be written to your immediate boss, be a short as possible, and include relevant factual data. It should also include a "statement of appreciation" about the opportunity you've had with the company. Be sure to keep a copy in your career portfolio for your own records.

# Put a Pretty Face on It

If this has been a good job and you are leaving for a better one, the goal is for everyone to be happy for you. If this was not a good job, no matter how awful or how unhappy you've been, the goal is still for everyone to be happy for you.

The easiest starting point is to let them know:

- You gave this decision serious thought (and perhaps that it was a difficult decision).
- You appreciate the opportunity you've had with the organization (company, department) you are leaving.
- You have learned a lot.
- You value the relationships you have built and look forward to keeping in touch.

Speak genuinely and from the heart. Even if you worked for the worst boss ever, it is still true that you learned a lot from your supervisor—even if it was only how *not* to manage a project or how *not* to treat people. The best way for people to be happy for you is to make them feel valued and appreciated. What? You say you worked for Attila the Hun? If someone asks you about the experience, say something along the lines of, "It was an experience I'll never forget," or "I learned a lot about territory expansion."

This is not the time to be angry about your experience or to use this as an opportunity to vent about all the things that are wrong with the company, the job, or the people you work with. Guess what? Since you are leaving, no one cares. And, if you behave unprofessionally, they might not even give you your going away party.

Now, enjoy your cake and get on with your future!

# ABOUT MARKETING:

# RESUMES AND COLLATERAL MATERIAL

# Misconceptions about Resumes

**CONVENTIONAL WISDOM:** Resumes get read, resumes get jobs, and there is a right way to write a resume.

**NEW THINKING:** A resume is necessary but not sufficient, and a good resume is designed for the reader.

If you think your resume isn't getting the job done for you, it might be because you don't understand resumes. On a regular basis, we encounter three common misconceptions about resumes that get in the way of successfully completing a job search.

# Misconception #1: Resumes get read.

Well, they might . . . eventually. But in order for a resume to get read, it needs to get selected. Put yourself in the shoes of a recruiter or a hiring manager. Your resume comes to them in a big pile of resumes (printed or electronic)—anywhere from 25 to 200 or more—often on a daily basis. Since they are not going to "read" that many resumes, their first step is to figure out what resumes to pay attention to. That means that the first and most important step in the resume process is to get your resume *selected*. If you have ever hired anyone, see if this process resonates with you. You take the group of resumes and start to go through them, sorting them into three categories: Yes, Maybe, No (or directly to the trash). It proceeds like this, with only a few seconds per resume: no, no, no, no, yes, no, no, no, no, no, maybe, no, no, no, no, no, no, no, no, no, maybe, no, no, no, no, no, no, yes, no, no, no. . .

What gets a resume selected? First, obvious fit for the job requirements. Do the key skills and experience jump off the page to the reader? Second, appearance. Is the resume neat, professional, readable, and without spelling mistakes? Third, valued characteristics that set the candidate apart. Does the candidate have a background at a prestigious company, outstanding education, clear record of accomplishments, and logical career progression? To see how "selectable" your resume is, try this test. Put your resume on your desk. Glance at it. What do you see? Would you pick it out of a pile of 50 resumes to read?

A similar process takes place when a recruiter electronically sorts through resumes received from postings or in searching databases, albeit with more emphasis on pre-selected keywords that show up "in context" in the body of the resume. Either way, you still have to get selected first.

# Misconception #2: Resumes get jobs.

If we had a dollar for every person who told us, "I've sent out lots of resumes, but I haven't gotten any calls," we'd be very rich indeed. *Resumes do not get jobs.* Your resume helps you get a job. In sales, a brochure is a key piece of marketing collateral. The dictionary defines collateral as "additional to and in support of something; accompanying or additional but secondary." The point is that when you are looking for a job, you are the product, and your resume is your marketing collateral. How much do you think you would sell by simply dropping off a 12-page glossy brochure? In effect, that is what you are doing when you just send out your resume.

You still need a good resume. Your resume, done properly, may get someone's attention. But more likely, you need to get someone's attention, and then back it up with your resume. That's when they are ready to dig into the details. What does get jobs is effective networking, a well-planned, well-executed job search, good interviewing skills, and a great professional self-presentation. Yes, having a good resume is essential to the process but not sufficient.

Some people may need to have a bio in addition to a resume. A bio is also marketing collateral and serves as a lead-in document. It is an interest-getter that is especially useful in the networking process. In initial sales calls, the representative often starts with a short introductory or "leave behind" flyer—just enough to cover the highlights—because until he or she has the customer's interest in the product or service, there is absolutely no interest in the detailed features.

Do you see the parallel with your resume and bio? Do you need to change your approach?

# Misconception #3: There is a right way to write a resume.

Everyone is an expert when it comes to resumes. Every recruiter, hiring manager, career consultant, author, and your older brother all believe they have the one magic formula. No matter what anyone tells you, they have not been handed the "truth." There is no magic formula. But common sense helps.

Common sense tells us that no matter what you believe or anyone else tells you about resume writing, the person who has the job has the final word. You want to get hired, not win a contest about the correct way to write a resume. If you know or find out that a recruiter or hiring manager wants a one-page resume, write a one-page resume.

Here are a few common sense guidelines for resumes:

1. Use a standard font in an easily readable point size.

2. Make your name big enough to be picked out of a stack of papers.

3. Leave 1-inch margins all the way around.

4. Include your name and page number—contact information optional—on any pages after the first page. If your name is not on the second or subsequent pages and printed pages get separated—for example, at the copier—there is no way for the lost pages to get re-attached correctly.

5. Depending on your audience and work history, your resume may be 1 to 3 pages. Just make sure that what's on all the pages adds real value.

6. Create an easy-to-read "unformatted" (often called "text") version for uploading to Internet job postings and other places where the resume will go into a large, searchable database.

7.  For hard copy, good quality white or ivory paper makes the best professional presentation. Make sure the color is light enough to copy well.

8.  No spelling mistakes.

9.  Use a positioning summary followed by a simple chronological format. No one will read your resume if they have to work too hard to piece it together. Watch an experienced recruiter. They go to the most recent job and start reading there. If your job information doesn't start until page two, you have wasted an entire page of prime real estate.

These guidelines reflect our understanding, at this moment in time, of effective resume design. Changes in the job market, technology, regulations, and hiring company processes continue to shape and inform our recommendations. There are also many opinions as to the best practices for resumes, and no one has the only right answer. Not even us.

# Job Search and Resumes Today

## WHAT'S IN and WHAT'S OUT

### INs

- Positioning statements
- Professional bios
- Comprehensive LinkedIn profiles
- Customized LinkedIn URLs included on resumes, business cards, and email signatures
- Key Words in Context (KWC)
- Email signatures with contact info on initial and reply messages
- Resume addendums for projects, deals, and other details
- Links to electronic portfolios on resumes of creative professionals
- White or ivory paper for printed resumes

### OUTs

- Self-serving or generic objectives
- Functional resumes
- Keyword lists
- Hobbies and interests
- Personal information
- "References upon request" on resumes
- Grey or colored paper for printed resumes
- Physical reference letters

# Resume Design as Marketing Communications

CONVENTIONAL WISDOM: Your resume is a marketing document.

NEW THINKING: Your resume is a marketing communications document.

It is pretty well accepted within the career coaching and resume writing industry that your resume is a marketing document. In other words, your resume is a document that needs to sell you and help you "put your best foot forward." That means your resume should reflect your strengths, skills, knowledge, and education. It may also mean the use of interesting color, graphics, and design to get your resume more attention.

In theory, this makes perfect sense. But in practice, this approach simply does not get to the heart of the matter.

# Business vs. Creative

Let's start by distinguishing between business resumes and creative resumes. Most people use business resumes, 1- to 2-page typed documents in Microsoft Word or in PDF format. Creative resumes are used by a small number of people who work in creative fields such as advertising, graphic design, and marketing. Creative resumes are actually "portfolio pieces" that display individuals' creative talents by incorporating their backgrounds, experiences, and education into graphic or artistic presentations. Visual concepts, color, and font choice are critical—and done by the individuals themselves to display their capabilities, not by hiring other professionals (graphic designers) to create their resumes.

# Mastering Marcom

A resume for a typical business professional or executive is 1 to 2 well-designed pages in a standard font, possibly with an addendum. Assuming you are writing your resume for a human being rather than a computer (which has its own special considerations), resume design must be about structuring content and displaying information on the page for clear messaging and communication. In business, this is called marketing communications, or "marcom," and covers everything from brochures to websites to flyers to social media presence.

In developing this type of resume, the most important point to remember is that you are writing for a customer. You are selling to that customer, and the product you are selling is you. Where this gets tricky is ensuring that the product—once again, you—solves the problem or issue the customer is having.

To that end, you must craft your resume with their needs in mind. No matter how proud you are of your accomplishments, if they are not aligned with the customer's needs and wants, they are probably not important. You always should be asking, "What does my NEXT employer care about?"

# Structure Strategy

This leads to structuring the document. How much attention should be paid to each job? It is not an equal opportunity document. Is your current job the most important? That depends. Have you only been in it for two months? Was it a bust or segue in your career not reflecting your desired next move?

What needs to show up on the first page? It's a fair bet that if you haven't caught the reader's interest on page one, he or she won't make it to the second. Ask yourself these questions:

- ▶ Does the display of information draw the reader's eye to the right place?
- ▶ Do I need to group certain jobs together?
- ▶ What is the right order for my accomplishment bullets?
- ▶ Do I need to group accomplishments under a single job?
- ▶ What is the best way to highlight performance results?
- ▶ Are the headings overwhelming the content?

A mockup of an effective brochure, for example, is laid out by defining the space where information will appear. Text is in a made-up language that delineates where it will go, how much there will be, and what size it will be in. If you think of your resume as a brochure in which you are designing and writing to a space, you can build a framework for an effective presentation.

The best resumes capture the imagination and interest of the recruiters or hiring managers and trigger their motivation to "buy."

## The Fresh New Face of Recruiting

Check out this excerpt from a recent position posting by an up-and-coming Internet retailer:

*What's the best job in the company? That's Lead Cheesecake Eater. Man, that guy has it made. But close behind is the person who creates the list of product features. They take builds from start to finish and are dead center in between all the departments, taking crap from Purchasing, Product Management, Operations and those jokers in Creative who do the write-ups. For a job like this, where you're gonna be taking responsibility for writing and editing product features and technical specifications as well as adhering to format, content and style guidelines, giving consideration to usability and ensuring accuracy, consistency and quality, you gotta be comfortable with all sorts of worsd. See? If you were here now, we wouldn't have made that mistake. Because a successful candidate like you will have great attention to detail and a strong work ethic.*

This description is followed by a traditional list of job duties and responsibilities. And they fit you to a tee! After you LOL and relax, having enjoyed a bit of levity in your otherwise boring and unsatisfying job search, what do you do about it?

The position description reflects the company's campy culture, but it's no joke. There are well defined responsibilities and competencies required. Your challenge is to respond in a way that captures not only your actual qualifications but also your personality and fit for the environment.

Here are our recommendations:

1. Take advantage of your cover letter or email transmittal letter to match the clever tone of the creative portion of the job description. Imagine yourself in a brilliant repartee with the author.

2. Since cover letters are often not read, you will also want to carry your humor through to your resume. The top of the first page where we recommend a "positioning" section—or where you may already have a profile or summary—can be converted into a short, carefully crafted and witty response.

3. Even though the job description is entertaining, it is very clear as to the nature and challenges of the work—what you need to know and what you need to do to be successful. It is rich in important keywords (like usability, technical specifications, and style guidelines) that need to be reflected back to the company and its computer.

4. Finally, just as this posting morphs into a traditional job description, you will need to respond with something more serious too. You need an excellent resume that lays out your experience, competencies, and contributions, as always. They are not trying to hire a buffoon. They just want to get you engaged with a little humor.

# Begin with the Audience in Mind

> **CONVENTIONAL WISDOM**: Resumes are for showing off what you've done.
>
> **NEW THINKING**: The person reading your resume wants to know: "What can you do for my company?" "Why should I pay you all this money?" "Why should I trust you to do this job?"

**P**erhaps the most frequently asked questions by clients developing resumes revolve around determining what should be included. We can't say too often or in too many ways, "What does your customer care about?" Whether it is your positioning at the top, the description of employers or jobs, your accomplishments, or credentials, every piece of information on your resume should be filtered through the screen of the audience you are writing for—your next employer.

## Sales 101

Your resume is a marketing document. Anyone in sales will tell you that the customer cares about one thing: what's in it for them. Yet even those experienced and successful in sales seem to forget this reality when writing their own resumes: never go to your customer selling what you want to sell. A good resume should lead your customer down the path to what they want to buy—hopefully you.

The key is understanding what the customer wants to buy and then aligning your-self—your experience, your accomplishments, your personal characteristics—with that. A person with a great list of accomplishments without a customer focus is essentially saying to the hiring company, "Look at all the great things I have done. What job do you have for me?" No matter how proud you are of an accomplishment or how great a skill you have, it is not relevant unless it relates to the job that needs to be done. Also, keep in mind that you cannot create a great resume if you don't know what you are looking for in a job. All you are saying is, "OMG! Please give me a job."

## It's Not Really About You

Unfortunately, most people talk about themselves on their resumes with an inward focus, an emphasis on their career history and details of their accomplishments—their view of what is important. It's a great biography but not a good customer-facing document. Newsflash! The resume is not all about you. It's only about you *in the context of* what the customer is interested in buying.

We call this your "Positioning." In marketing, positioning means the process by which marketers try to create an image or identity in the minds of their target markets for their products, brands, or organizations. Positioning is extremely useful for describing the alignment of your talents with the needs of the organization and highlighting the value of your contributions. That is, after all, how the match will be made.

## Where Does Branding Fit In

Building "brands" for job-seekers is a popular pastime for career consultants, authors, and speakers these days. In our opinion, however, most of these experts are confusing branding and positioning. People in a career transition or job search should be more concerned with positioning than branding. Small business owners have the more complicated task of determining whether the focus needs to be on branding or positioning, for themselves or their businesses, or all of these.

A brand, in contrast to positioning, is the identity of a specific product, service, or business as reflected in a name, sign, symbol, color combination, or slogan. A legally protected brand name is called a trademark or service mark.

The most effective personal brands usually reflect a complete metaphor. Here are some powerful examples we've encountered.

- Corporate Chiropractor: Helping align a corporation from top to bottom
- Flying Ace in the World of IT Leadership: Piloting innovation to benefit the bottom line
- Corporate Athlete: Helping companies cross the finish line
- Renaissance Woman: Serving HR and the company across various disciplines and issues

When all is said and done, branding is a piece of the puzzle, but a positioning statement is much more likely to get you the match you desire.

## Identifying Positioning Keywords

When a job search starts, hiring managers have a few key items that are essential to their hiring decisions. This list may be conscious or unconscious ("I'll know it when I see it"). And frequently, this list is not exactly the same as position-standard skill sets. Who is this person really trying to hire? What are the skills and characteristics that make a difference to the hiring manager? You will want to create a short list of keywords that align, as best they can, with them. If you don't match up perfectly, it's okay to ignore what's missing. A good place to start your research is by carefully reading job postings or gathering other information about this or similar positions.

Many of the jobs you apply for may need small modifications to your resume to effectively sell yourself. That doesn't mean you have to create entirely different resumes for each position. For a good multi-purpose resume, create a basic resume based on a few specific jobs you might want. Then manipulate it a little bit according to your audience when you can. Remember, there is always a customer out there. Your job is to identify what the customer wants to buy and sell yourself.

# Skills-Based, Functional Resumes Are Obsolete

> **CONVENTIONAL WISDOM:** Use a functional resume to highlight your talents and transferrable skills.
>
> **NEW THINKING:** Do not—DO NOT—use a functional resume ever, especially when looking for a career change or where there are gaps or issues in your experience. You are not fooling anyone.

Creating an appealing resume when seeking a career change, or when you have problematic segues or discontinuities in your career history, is quite challenging. In an attempt to address this, "functional resumes" were created more than 50 years ago by outplacement companies to highlight transferrable skills. A functional resume, the opposite of a chronological resume, highlights specific competencies, accomplishments, and leadership skills. It is designed so that a resume reader doesn't see where a person has worked until halfway down the page or on page two.

## A Good Idea in Theory, But . . .

In practice, people who are hiring hate functional resumes. Just ask recruiters and hiring managers, and they won't hesitate to tell you about their overwhelming dislike of functional resumes. In fact, many recruiters will tell you that as soon as they see a functional resume they think, "What are they hiding?" You might as well throw your resume in the waste basket yourself. Reconstructing a deconstructed functional resume isn't worth the recruiter's time. Keep in mind that functional resumes were created by people who weren't actually hiring.

Functional resumes are usually structured with categorized and bulleted lists of accomplishments—such as communication skills, sales skills, or leadership skills—which typically take up half or more of the resume. The career history, which shows employers, jobs, and dates, is typically crammed at the bottom. The intent is to put the focus on capabilities and contributions, while minimizing either (a) the lack of connection between the individual's prior career and the new direction; or (b) a mediocre or inconsistent job progression.

## Three Steps to an Effective Chronological Resume

Recruiters and managers may not like functional resumes, but they don't like discontinuities either. Yet many job seekers have blips in their resumes that must be dealt with. Since we've already established that functional resumes are a no-no, what can job seekers with less than perfect career paths do within the context of a chronological resume?

Follow these three steps:

1.  Structure your resume to get your message across. You can use "functional" groupings of responsibilities and accomplishments within the context of a particular job.

2.  Carefully select the responsibilities and accomplishments that best reflect your transferrable skills, and make sure those stand out. You may need to revisit all your jobs, dig out the competencies that are related to the job you are targeting, and focus on those as you reconstruct your career history.

3.  Review significant professional and community activities that give you an opportunity to showcase these skills and close career gaps.

What should emerge are themes that are relevant to your next job or new career direction. You might consider bolding or highlighting certain information to make the themes more visible.

In the case where your prior work experience does not support your new career direction, consider adding the word "Objective" to the headline in your profile or positioning section. That helps to signal the reader that there may be a disconnect between what you are targeting and the career history that follows. Even though, as a general rule, objective statements are self-serving and should be avoided at all costs, this is one situation when we advocate using them.

So, don't be lured by a functional resume. If you have a problematic career history or are changing fields, the resume alone is not going to be the primary source of generating interest anyway. Rather, it needs to serve as a compelling "back story" for when you get someone to talk to you through networking and pursuing introductions and other connections.

# The Right Length for a Resume

CONVENTIONAL WISDOM: There is a right length for a resume. It has to be one page. It has to be two pages. Longer is better. A three-page resume is taboo.

NEW THINKING: Nothing is taboo if you present it correctly.

Regarding the length of a resume, there is no area of resume writing in which people are surer about their opinions, and there are more opinions than we can count. As a general rule, but not a mandate, a resume should be no longer than one or two pages. That said, a three-page resume isn't taboo. In fact, nothing is taboo if you present it correctly. It all depends on how your information is laid out, and whether what you are including adds value.

## Keep it (Relatively) Short

In general, business resumes are one—three pages. Two pages are standard for senior level professionals and executives. Entry level candidates, highly specialized professionals, and occasionally very senior executives may have one-page resumes. Once in a while three pages are needed to cover relevant and significant accomplishments in early career positions. Recruiters of senior technical talent do not seem to mind longer resumes, but this is an exception to the norm.

Also, not all jobs are equal. Older or less interesting jobs should have less attention and less "real estate" than current or more important jobs. Be sure to understand what information is going to be most relevant to the reader, especially for the initial screener. If you can consolidate information without excluding anything important, then do it. If your resume really needs three pages, then by all means present it that way.

## When to Use Addendums

If you work in an industry that includes large-scale projects—for example, IT or engineering projects, consulting engagements, financial deals, court cases, large scale construction projects—detailed information may need to be pulled out of the resume and included in an addendum. Addendums are also useful for lengthy lists of professional affiliations, numerous publications, speaking engagements, or media coverage. The addendum can be an integral part of the resume as a third page, or it can be a separate document. Occasionally, you could have more than one addendum.

Addendums can also be created and organized for specific audiences. The items can be chosen based on what is most relevant by industry, project type, or size. Key information can be displayed in the main resume.

## Curriculum Vitae (CV) vs. Resume

Unless you live in Europe, where CVs are really a blend of a CV and a resume, a CV and a resume are two different things. In the United States, a CV is a credentialing document that is used by academics, scientists, and researchers to document their education, grants, publications, speaking engagements, projects, where they've worked, and who they've worked with and under. An accomplished academic could have a CV of five to fifteen pages—or even more—if they have been a prolific writer and speaker.

So, when it comes to resumes, short is sweet, but not at the expense of leaving out crucial information.

# Lopping off the Early Years

When it comes to what you should include on your resume and what you shouldn't, there is a widely held belief these days that only the most recent 10 or 15 years are important. The thinking is that you aren't likely to be hired on information based that far in the past. And since the information isn't relevant anyway, lopping off your early career might be a good way to get your resume down to two pages.

## Keep Imaginations in Check

If you think that those years don't matter, think again. If you simply remove anything except the most current 10 or 15 years of your career, a recruiter or hiring manager will know something is missing and wonder what you're trying to hide.

For example, if the earliest job on your resume is "Director of Marketing," the recruiter is well aware that you didn't come out of the womb into a position at that level. Unwittingly, you have engaged the recruiter's imagination. He or she is left wondering, "What happened?" "Where were you?" and "What were you doing?" Human nature will fill the void with the worst possible scenarios. Were you in rehab? Did you do a stint behind bars? Are you 93 years old?

Unfortunately, leaving your early career off your resume focuses the reader's attention on the part of the resume that rightfully should get the least attention. Instead of having the reader focus on your current roles and contributions–which is your original intention and at least part of the reason why you left your early years off in the first place—the reader gets stuck somewhere in the netherworld of your old history. You have just been sabotaged by your own good intentions.

## Consolidate, Don't Eliminate

So, what can you do to ensure the focus remains on the right stuff? Don't eliminate. Instead, consolidate. Your resume is not an "equal opportunity" document. You may find the best way is to simply list companies and job titles in chronological order, with or without dates, without lengthy descriptions. You can also summarize jobs in a couple of sentences; for example, "progressed through the ranks of IBM's financial organization, ultimately achieving the position of Accounting Manager." If you had a great accomplishment during this time, you can write about it in an additional sentence, for example "Twice received the *Spotlight Award* for leadership excellence in 1996 and 1998." This section can also be provided with or without dates, especially if your age is an issue.

Keep the reader focused where you want them. Avoid the specter of unrequited curiosity by including enough information to keep the reader from fixating on what's missing.

# Read the Instructions

CONVENTIONAL WISDOM: Job postings are used for applying to jobs.

NEW THINKING: Job postings and position specifications provide an awesome source of market intelligence that can help focus your job search and dramatically improve your resume.

Employers are looking for people who closely match the specific requirements of a job. The more closely the employer (or its computer) perceives you match up, the more interest you will generate. The proliferation of job boards and corporate websites with job postings make it easy now to find out what employers want. For executives, getting position specifications from executive search recruiters serves the same purpose. So, when a headhunter calls, make sure to get the specifications and keep them for future reference, regardless of your interest at the moment in the particular job.

## How to Use Job Postings for Market Research

Job postings and specifications provide a surrogate for market research. Here's how to do it.

1.  Find three to five postings that meet the following criteria: a) you would be interested in the job, b) you believe you are qualified, and c) you believe

the employer would find you qualified. Don't worry about geography. For the purpose of research, it doesn't matter if the job is in your location or thousands of miles away.

2. Review each job with attention to job title, job responsibilities, candidate requirements, and the language the employer is using to describe those things. Also note any consistent themes among the various jobs. Now you have the instructions for writing your resume and the answer sheet for what should be included.

3. Use your research to create or modify your resume and cover letter to reflect the target jobs as they have been described by the hiring companies. Select relevant key words to be included.

When doing your research, keep in mind that not everything in a job description is important. Some information included by HR relates to job grade considerations and adherence to legal compliance. Sometimes a job description is an agglomeration of "everything but the kitchen sink" that someone (or multiple someones) think the perfect candidate should have. Go through the job description and mark those items you believe are key to the person they are *really* trying to hire. Also, be cautious of words like leadership, communication, and interpersonal skills. Every employer says they want them, and every candidate says they have them. Try to glean explicitly what type, for example, of communications skills the employer is seeking. Are they talking about presentation skills, client communications, or managing employees?

There is an added benefit to this exercise. Some people discover that the job they thought they were looking for doesn't exist, that it doesn't pay what they expected, or that they are not sufficiently qualified to be a serious contender. Now they have the opportunity to redirect their job search plans appropriately.

# Ask Not "What Can My Employer Do for Me?"

CONVENTIONAL WISDOM: All resumes should contain an Objective stating what a candidate wants from the job.

NEW THINKING: Self-serving objectives are outdated and have no place on the resume.

Many job applicants typically place an "objective" area at the top of their resumes. Objectives frequently communicate something like, "I want a great job with a great company with excellent pay and benefits where I can use my superior skills and unique talents."

While it may be nice for you to define your goals, at this point in the job-seeking process, employers simply don't care what's in it for you. They are not in the social work business (unless, of course, you are applying for a social work position). Employers hire because they have specific needs. They want an appropriately qualified person who can hit the ground running and get the job done.

That's not to say your goals and objectives are irrelevant. Your goals, objectives, and the things that motivate you are relevant at other times, such as during the interview process, just not on your resume.

Employers want to know what you can do for them. As a general rule, instead of an objective, include a headline along with a positioning statement that focuses on your contributions or, at the very least, your skills. This positioning statement should answer questions like, "Who are you?" "What talents do you bring to the table?" and "How can you contribute to the company?"

## Exception to the Rule

The one exception to this rule is using an objective when there is some kind of disconnect between the jobs you are applying for and your career history. Let's say you have been in accounting, but now want to do sales. Clearly, your work history will not reflect sales. You want to help the resume reader connect the dots between accounting and sales by using an objective. In this case, your objective might be "Objective: Accounting Software Sales."

# Keyword Magic

> **Conventional Wisdom**: The way to beat database searches is to have the "right" buzzwords for your industry or job in your resume and in a core competency list.
>
> **New Thinking**: Keywords need to be aligned with your target jobs and integrated into your experience with sufficient density that they will show up in the body of your resume multiple times during a database search.

Y ou've probably been told that recruiters use keywords to pick resumes out of the many they receive online or store in their Applicant Tracking Systems (ATS). That's true. They do "parameter driven searches." In other words, they type in relevant keywords and run them against their databases to find resumes with those keywords. And they want to see those keywords in the context of your real experience, not just on lists. This is referred to as Keywords in Context (KWC).

## Why You Can't Beat the System

Let's say a recruiter for the airline industry is looking for a manager in their revenue accounting department. The recruiter might type in "revenue accounting manager" and "airline." Perhaps the systems find 5,000 or so resumes, so then the recruiter narrows the search by adding a specific geography, say Florida. To further refine the search, the recruiter might add a college degree or other criteria to the search parameters. Most systems highlight search terms on the resumes it selects, often in yellow. The recruiter will look for how much "yellow" is on the page as well as how often their specific search terms, or keywords, show up. In more sophisticated systems, it may give the resume a ranking as to how well it matches the search criteria.

While this sounds quite technical, searches are ultimately conducted by humans, not computers. Computers do what they are told to do, and it is the recruiter who is issuing the instructions. They are choosing the keywords. And every recruiter will do it somewhat differently. So, in the end, you can't second guess the vagaries of human behavior.

Furthermore, Applicant Tracking Systems have embedded "intelligence" in the form of complex algorithms to determine which resumes it selects once the keywords have been entered. So, unless you plan to work for a company that develops this software, your time is better spent elsewhere than decoding the rules.

A little help is on the way, but still it's in its infancy. Software is being developed that will let you do a trial run of your resume against a specific position description. With this analysis, you can make adjustments to your resume to increase your odds. Over time, these applications will become more reliable and accessible to the mainstream.

## How to Increase the Odds

Put yourself in the position of the recruiter. Given the company and the job, what keywords do you think the recruiter is most likely to search for? Those are your "hot words." It's possible that you have no idea what keywords they will search for. That's okay.

There are two ways you can find out. First, if you know a resume writer or recruiter, they may be able to help. Many regularly use lists of keywords for certain types of industries, professions, and jobs. Alternatively, you might be able to find a prepared list of keywords in an Internet search.

Second, you can create your own list by researching postings on the job boards or company websites. The job descriptions will usually offer up consistent themes, descriptors, words, and language that you should incorporate into your keyword list. They can be found in the job titles, job responsibilities, and applicant qualifications.

Is one way better than the other? In our opinion, researching keywords from real job postings is much more effective than getting them from a generic list. The keywords will be more targeted and better aligned with the jobs you are interested in.

Once you've developed your key words, include them multiple times in the body of your resume. For example, a project manager shared her resume with us, and we discovered that the words "project manager" never actually showed up in the entire resume! So, we went back and made some changes. For example, where her job description said "Led the team that developed. . . ," we changed the wording to "Served as project manager for the team that developed. . . ." You get the idea. It is, of course, important to represent your roles and responsibilities accurately.

Another common mistake is that job seekers concentrate on how they do their jobs. While it's fine to include terms such as "creative solution," "transformation," or "proven track record," they should not be confused with keywords. Recruiters would never search on these terms. Rather, they search on specifics such as industry (airline, retail, telecommunications), function (accounting, engineering, IT), knowledge (SEC reporting, lean manufacturing, electronic medical records), or experience (program management, e-commerce, branding). You should include the complete terms as well as their commonly used acronyms (electronic medical records and EMR; project management professional and PMP).

Recruiters search social media sites with keywords as well. So in addition to your resume, important keywords must show up there often enough for you to be found.

## Don't Lose Sleep over Your Keywords

While keywords play an important role on your resume, don't lose sleep over them. Recruiters frequently use keyword searches to narrow down the plethora of applicants. But you've still got Vegas odds. Some people spend hours honing their keywords and still don't get contacted. Do the best you can but don't agonize. A reasonable strategy is to make a good effort to get solid keywords into your resume, but not waste your time trying to figure out the perfect ones. The odds of your resume being the winner in a database search, despite your best efforts, are still pretty small.

# Honesty Is the Best Policy

**CONVENTIONAL WISDOM**: Lying on resumes is most often intentional with severe consequences for those who get caught.

**NEW THINKING**: Outright lying on resumes typically has consequences, but the vast majority of incidents are embellishments or misrepresentations because job seekers don't know how to present information correctly.

As career coaches who help many people develop their resumes and bios, structure their messages, and put their "best foot forward," our #1 rule is NEVER LIE.

Lies catch up with you. They compromise your personal integrity, as well as the market's perception of the integrity and judgment of the people who have hired or will hire you. This is a lose-lose situation for everyone. If you can't get the job based on who you really are, find another job or fix your credentials—get a degree, work more years in the field, or get certified.

Many well-intentioned people simply don't know how to describe themselves articulately or structure information to communicate clearly. There are four main places where misrepresentation takes place: credentials, job titles, credit for work or contributions, and employers.

# Credentials

Expect your credentials to be verified, especially college degrees. To that end, make sure all information pertaining to your degree—program of study, name of university—is accurate and correct. If you don't have a degree, don't say so. It's that simple. Companies that do verify will request your authorization so they can obtain that information. If they don't verify, don't think you're home free. There are many circumstances that could cause your lack of degree to come to light later, which could be the cause for embarrassment, termination, or worse.

If you have some college or have inactive licenses or certifications, they can add value to your credentials. For example, if you attended college but did not finish, you can write *John Alma University, Chemistry program, 1999—2001*, to show that you attended. If you are currently in a degree program, you can write *Great Plains University, MBA expected 20XX*. If you have previously held credentials that are no longer active, just say so, for example, *Top Secret Security Clearance (inactive)* or *Tennessee Real Estate License (inactive)*. This shows you know the stuff and once passed the test, adding credibility to your knowledge and abilities.

Some other examples include:

- *Six Sigma Black Belt expected 20XX*
- *Essentials of Business Analysis, Villanova University, Certificate Expected August 20XX*
- *Pre-Med Program, University of Texas at Austin, 105 credit hours*
- *Graduate Business Management Courses, California State University at Hayward*
- *Completed all coursework (60 hours) required for Texas Real Estate License*

# Job Titles

Verification of employment is often automated today, so it is especially important that the titles on your resume, especially that of your current or mosr recent job, match exactly what HR has in its records. If you have an unusual title or one that doesn't communicate your role effectively, you can always add some descriptive terminology as long as it truly reflects the job you were doing, for example, Manager of Operations Staff [official title] and Acting Director, Lean Manufacturing [additional descriptive information]. On the other hand, if you had a "Manager" title, changing the title to "Director" or "VP" or any other title you think you ought to have had is considered a fraudulent practice. If you don't think your title correctly reflects your level of responsibility, you may be able to make the point by noting who you reported to, for example, "Reporting directly to the Chief Marketing Officer, . . ."

# Credit

Does it belong to you or to someone else? If you use the word "I," frequently—I did this and I did that— you'll raise a red flag. However, using the word "we" too much—we did this and we did that—is equally as suspect. In one case, you are likely to be tagged as arrogant and unable to recognize the contributions of others. In the other case, you will likely to be tagged as a "wimp" who is lacking in leadership abilities, is without personal contributions to the organization, or is afraid to take credit for accomplishments. If it is yours, own it. Here's an example: *Achieved the highest sales record in 2012."* If you don't fully own something, at least present your role in the accomplishment. You might say something like *Led the team that achieved the highest sales record in 2012.*

When it comes to credit, there are lots of gray areas. If you're wondering if you should take credit for an achievement, a good test is whether your boss would agree with what you are claiming. Even if you think you and your boss wouldn't agree—for example, because you believe you were actually doing his/her job—your resume is not the place to make that point or disrespect your boss. Stick with politically correct ways to describe what you did that still reflect your exceptional contributions.

# Employers

This situation comes up most frequently for people who worked on contract either independently or through a third-party firm. When presenting your employment, make it clear who you actually worked for, which may be different than who you did the work for. For example, if you were contracted to Microsoft to work on a project, you did not work for Microsoft. If you are uncertain or confused as to your actual employer, simply take a look at your paycheck. The company that pays you is the one you work for. If you have contracted independently, you will have invoiced the company for the work and received a 1099 at the end of the year. Avoid leading the reader to the conclusion that you actually worked for a company when you were not on the payroll. This will be immediately obvious when someone tries to verify your employment, and the company has no record of you.

We advocate these ways to correctly list contract work on your resume:

- ▶ List the third party as your employer and show the work as an "assignment" at the company you are contracted to.
- ▶ List the company you are contracted to, and at the beginning of your job description state you worked on contract through the third party.
- ▶ If you have worked for many different third party firms for short periods of time, which is common in technical contracting, group the assignments to facilitate understanding of your work history as a contractor.
- ▶ Use "Independent Contractor" or your own company name as your employer if you have contracted independently, and show the work as an "engagement."

The adage "honesty is the best policy" holds true in many areas of our lives, including the areas related to our careers. Resist the urge to misrepresent, embellish, or outright lie on your resume. It's more trouble now or in the future than it's worth.

# Truth or Dare? Dealing with Gaps in Your Job History

CONVENTIONAL WISDOM: Use a functional resume or handle it in your cover letter.

NEW THINKING: Camouflage the gap wherever you can. Then have a crisp, honest strategy for the rest.

Gaps in your resume? Oh, no! While employment gaps are frowned upon by recruiters, there are lots of reasons why you might have gaps on your resume.

- ▶ Time out to raise children
- ▶ Caring for elderly parents or family illnesses
- ▶ Personal health issues
- ▶ Additional education
- ▶ Intentional leave of absence (mission work, traveling around the world)
- ▶ Laid off and between jobs
- ▶ Fired because of improprieties you conducted or with which you were associated
- ▶ Incarceration (yes, this one is really tricky)

Because employers and recruiters often have an instant negative reaction to obvious gaps, you must have a sound and well thought out strategy for presenting your background both in your resume and during the interview process. Since there are wide ranging reasons a person might be out of work for an extended period of time, the solutions will also vary depending on the situation. There are, however, some general guidelines that will help you minimize the potential damage or discomfort, and help you become more confident and successful throughout the process.

## Five Options for Putting Your Best Foot Forward

Here are five options for creating the right first impression on your resume. What you do will depend on your specific circumstances. You might even use a combination of these strategies.

1. ***Years only.*** Display only years of your employment, not months. Employers really don't care about a few months here or there. They want to see a continuous flow of experience. By leaving out months, you can easily seam up several months of unemployment.

2. ***Consolidate early years.*** If your employment gap was a number of years ago, it can be camouflaged within a summary of earlier experience and accomplishments, typically more than 10 or 15 years ago. Consolidate early years to avoid inflaming the curiosity of the reader. Instead, provide enough information to complete the story. Here are some examples:

---

*For a current Vice President of Sales:*

EARLIER CAREER (consistent format as company name)   [With or without years]

Held positions in sales and sales management at [Company A] and [Company B]. Consistently ranked in top 10% of producers.

---

> *For a current Director of a Regional Symphony:*
>
> Previous Experience: Held college and high school teaching positions with College A, College B, and the Metroplex Independent School District. Also served as instructor with the Metroplex Summer Musicals School and as a private voice teacher.

> *For a radio station Account Executive*
>
> PRIOR POSITIONS                                      [With or without years]
>
> Held office management positions with Accounting firms and Property Management companies

This might be the full story, or it might mask some issues. It doesn't have to include every company or every job. Even naming the companies is optional. If it gives you "pedigree," put their names in. Regardless, it fills in the gaps in the story and takes attention away from what happened far in the past, which is not what an employer is hiring you for anyway.

3.  ***Contract or Part-time Work.*** Include any freelance work, consulting, or part-time work in your experience. Include the name of the organization, job functions, years, and city and state. Treat this work as a regular job with appropriate caveats in the description so that it's not misleading. For the heading in this area, use "Experience" rather than "Job History" or "Work Experience."

> **Independent Sales Consultant, New York, NY** [Year—Year]
>
> *Client Company / Sales Development Manager*
>
> Chartered with building alliances and strategic partnerships for a start-up technology company. Responsible for developing and negotiating partner contracts, creating "go-to-market" campaigns, and training sales personnel on product features and benefits. Built and grew sales team from the ground up to $5 million in annual revenue in less than 2 years and transitioned the team from contract into an internal function.

4. *Unpaid work.* Include volunteer work, mentoring, or writing in your Experience section, with the appropriate acknowledgement of your unpaid status. This is more of a stretch, but these experiences may also fit in appropriately and be included on your resume chronologically. In this case, for your career history, use the heading "Experience." Be creative and dig deep to identify some of the relevant and productive things you did during any "dormant" period in your career history. It's possible that you can list them in a similar format as your other jobs—with job title, company name, job description, and dates—and include positive skills you used or sharpened.

> **St. Mary's Hospital, Denver, CO** [Year—Year]
>
> *Gift Shop Manager*
>
> Served as a volunteer responsible for the six-day operation of a gift shop in a large not-for-profit hospital. Responsibilities included sales, procurement, inventory management, accounting, budgeting, volunteer staffing and training, and vendor relations. With product realignment, innovative sourcing strategies, and targeted cost reductions, gift shop increased its contributions to $250,000 per year to the children's rehabilitation center.

5. ***Explain it.*** Introduce a short explanation at the beginning of your Experience section, in small font. In cases where you have been completely out of work for personal reasons, such as caring for elderly parents or sick children, your most recent job experience may be several years ago. You might choose to insert a short description of your time out of the work force, such as "*Since 2011, on sabbatical for personal family matters.*"

Remember, your resume is a marketing communications document that should emphasize your skills, capabilities, experiences, and unique talents to recruiters and potential employers. There are no hard and fast rules about what has to be included or not, how it should be presented, and what can or cannot be listed where. With issues like a significant experience gap, it's more important to communicate what value you bring to the job and, if possible, how you used your time. As long as you are truthful, even if it's well-crafted and carefully worded, you'll be fine.

# Now for the Interview

Let's say you've safely made it past the recruiting/screening gauntlet, and now you have the opportunity to present your skills and capabilities in an interview either in person or over the phone. There are two scenarios you can expect: 1) your resume can't fully camouflage your experience gap or 2) it can.

If the interviewer can't tell from your resume that you were unemployed for a few months, don't volunteer this information. Why would you want to sidetrack an interview with a discussion that can possibly create doubt or spend time on unproductive topics? Instead, focus on what is relevant and why you are a great candidate.

This is obviously the best-case scenario. More commonly, your resume may hint at a gap or just outright show one. Good interviewers are going to spot it and ask you about it. You must be prepared with a reasonable and credible explanation. Your comments should be brief, to the point, and not over-disclosing, unless in the rare situation it's to your advantage. Various life experiences and choices, like caring for a family or recovering from an injury, are not necessarily negative. As long as you remain poised, positive, and confident, you can sail past these hazards with aplomb. If you can tie in what you learned, what you accomplished personally, or any new skills you cultivated, even better.

But what if you were out of work for really negative reasons? In that case, there are a few more things you need to consider. The most important resource you have is the network of people who know you, trust you, and value what you can bring to the table. Their sponsorship and support can help you strengthen your credibility and job worthiness. Since networking is key for getting jobs, it is the super golden key for you. Then, as you progress in the screening and interviewing process, you must handle this negative circumstance early in the process and professionally. Nobody likes surprises, especially late in the game at the point of making the hiring decision.

No matter what the job gap circumstances, it is mandatory that you create a viable strategy to address them. Then, carefully manage your marketing materials, your scripts, and your story so that it all holds together, is truthful and credible, and still keeps you in the running in the best possible light.

# About That "Other Stuff" at the Bottom of Your Resume

---

**CONVENTIONAL WISDOM:** Employers love job candidates with community work, hobbies, and interests on their resumes to show they are well rounded and to provide ideas for "small talk."

**NEW THINKING:** Employers don't care about your hobbies and personal interests unless it is related to your job or demonstrates your leadership experience and accomplishments.

---

L et's cut to the chase. Hobbies, interests, and personal information do not belong on resumes today. Back in the day, interviewers often calibrated candidates based on social standing and connections, and many of them openly discriminated based on marital status. Today, nobody cares. And even if they do, they are not allowed to ask. The first rule is that if it can't be asked in an interview, it shouldn't be on your resume.

How do you know what can't be asked? Simple. If it's not *job related*, then it's not a legal question and shouldn't be asked. Keep your resume job related and don't cross into personal territory like how many years you've been happily married, ages of your children, church, or political affiliations.

# Keep Your Hobbies to Yourself

Hobbies are especially taboo. Unless you are applying for work at a company that manufacturers cat figurines, no one needs to know you collect these beauties. Comments like "enjoys golf, tennis, and stamp collecting" might be good conversation topics, but they absolutely don't belong on the resume. The only exception—and this is quite rare by the way—is *if* something about that particular activity is directly job related. For example, if you are applying for a business development role in financial services and you are a "scratch" golfer, you might put it on your resume because business development in this industry is common on the golf course. Don't call it a "hobby" though. Remember, employers don't care about your hobbies. Instead, create a "Credentials and Achievements" section and put "Award-winning golfer in X League" in that section.

# Share Community Service

Since resumes must be specifically job related and relevant, things like publications, board positions, and speaking engagements should be included. Further, as an increasing number of companies are valuing social responsibility and community involvement, including volunteer participation on your resume may be seen as a plus. We recommend using a separate section at the end of the resume following your education. A heading like "Community and Civic Activities" allows you to list your leadership roles and meaningful achievements outside of work. These entries should be limited to those professional and community activities that have bearing on the job and that show leadership or highlight expertise in your field.

For online applications, you may be limited in how you can display these activities. Most job boards enable you to upload your resume, so community service will be picked up exactly as you display it on your resume. However, some systems still require you to enter "jobs" one at a time. In these situations, we suggest adding another "job" and clearly identifying it as community service by putting "volunteer" in your job title. If you had a real title with the volunteer organization, it's acceptable to include it.

# Create Balance

Regardless of its importance and your contribution, most employers will consider community activities second. Keep descriptions short, accomplishment focused, and job relevant. For lesser-known organizations, help the reader by stating its purpose, for example Sunlight Foundation, advocates for adopting children with special needs. Carefully select activities that display leadership roles or specific accomplishments. Be very careful and strategic in using religious, political, or ethnic organizations. Normally we recommend leaving these off completely, but if you specifically want to convey a "message," then including something like "President of the Hispanic Chamber of Commerce" is an effective way to do this.

Even though employers may value community service, don't get carried away and make it seem as if you have another full-time job. Some employers might be concerned about hiring someone with too many extracurricular responsibilities. Also, too much community service could mean not enough time spent in professional development or industry activities. The best approach is to balance your volunteer time between professional, industry, and community organizations.

Some job seekers, like former homemakers returning to the workforce, may have minimal paid work experience but significant volunteer responsibilities and accomplishments. Honestly, as far as potential employers are concerned, being a volunteer is not as good as having a paid job. However, if that is the experience you have, then that's what you have. You can package your skills and hone your presentation to capitalize on what you do well. Just recognize that your job search strategy has to focus on finding opportunities through networking so that your resume becomes the "back story" rather than the "front story." Your success will depend on generating interest and interviews through the people you know and the people they know, rather than sending out a plethora of resumes.

All that "other stuff" at the bottom of your resume is important—so put thought into what you present. Be sure any information you include is relevant to the job. This is not the place to list "I like cooking" unless you're a nutritionist, dietician, or chef.

# Cover Letters Are Like Parsley

**CONVENTIONAL WISDOM**: Investing lots of time and energy in writing an exquisite cover letter will make all the difference in getting selected for an interview.

**NEW THINKING**: Cover letters matter but only to gift wrap your resume and provide the right first impression.

We have asked clients with hiring responsibilities and experienced recruiters we know what they do with cover letters. The consistent answer is "not much." Hiring managers often don't even get the cover letters, especially when resumes have been pre-selected by an internal or external recruiter.

## Why Include a Cover Letter?

Just like a fax cover sheet or a table of contents in a book, the cover letter is packaging and presentation. It needs to be there. You would never send a sales proposal or respond to an RFP without a cover letter. Most people don't spend much time with them, but they feel uncomfortable if they aren't there. A particular client who was trying to grasp this concept said, "I get it! Cover letters are like parsley. You put it on the plate to make it look nice, but no one eats it."

A key exception is recruiters who hire people for non-professional or entry level jobs. They often use cover letters to see if applicants can construct brief letters and write coherently. Of course, this is only a good test if the applicants have written the letter themselves—and even then the cover letter may have been substantially copied from a book. If you have trouble composing a letter or your English is not fluent, there are plenty of resources to help you write a good cover letter.

Some recruiters also say that they use the cover letter as an opportunity to see if applicants can "follow instructions." If the posting asks for a cover letter, did the applicant send one? Occasionally, cover letters are read to see if applicants have taken the time to understand the jobs and reflect that in terms of their own qualifications—and this is a good use of a cover letter.

The real value of the cover letter is to you. Each time you write one, you will personalize it and highlight your key qualifications for a particular job opportunity. As you think this through and condense your thoughts into a few bulleted points, you will gain fluency in aligning yourself with opportunities and in talking about yourself. And since it has a limited audience, it doesn't matter if you get it exactly right.

## Save Time, Reduce Anxiety

Think of all the money and time you will save and anxiety eliminated now that you understand the limited use of your cover letter. You don't need to buy and study books like *79 Killer Cover Letters Guaranteed to Get Jobs*. You can write your cover letter quickly and not lose any sleep over it.

Furthermore, you certainly don't want to "save" any important information for just your cover letter—get it into your resume, which hopefully is being read. In addition, a cover letter is not the place to convey your life story, personal information about your circumstances (I've been tending to a sick parent for the past 2 years), or anything else that distracts from your qualifications and interest in the job.

# Get It Right—Quickly and Efficiently

Your cover letter should be one page in an appropriately large point size and margins for a letter. Start by writing a cover letter formatted as a traditional letter that can be printed or sent as an email attachment. With minor modifications, it works equally well as the text of an email. If it is going to be printed or sent as an attachment, it should be in the same font as the resume that it is going with. If it is being included in the body of an email, whatever font and point size is the default for your email should be fine.

As a target, limit creation of your cover letter to 5—10 minutes. The more of them you do, the faster you will be able to create them. You will also find the right balance between repeatable information and that which needs to be personalized for each opportunity.

# Convert To Email

In an email, the contact information at the top, the date and inside address of a letter are not used. In addition, the "Dear" is omitted from the salutation. The body of the letter is exactly the same.

An email then requires a subject and a "signature". The subject should be simple and direct. Examples of appropriate subject lines are:

- ▶ Referred by (name)
- ▶ Job Board (name) Posting #12345, Job Title
- ▶ Job (title) Position (or Opportunity)
- ▶ As directed by a posting

If you are responding to a recruiter or a posting, include your name at the end of the subject line. It will make it easier for the recruiter to retrieve your response.

An email signature should be created for both an "initial" email and a "reply." Include your name, your phone number, and your email address. By including a signature on all replies, the recipient has immediate access to your contact information and in other cases doesn't have to go hunting through an email chain to find it. You're making it easy for someone to contact you.

# Cover Letter Guidelines

We recommend four short paragraphs for the cover letter body.

1. *Paragraph 1—Introduction and Statement of Value.* State the purpose for the letter and your statement of contribution personalized to the company and job. Mention personal connections if applicable.

2. *Paragraph 2—Qualification and Alignment.* Open with a statement like "My background and experience make me an excellent fit for the position." Then include a few bullets that summarize your key qualifications that align with the job requirements. Include here or in Paragraph 3 any obscure or special requirements that might be making this a difficult job to fill.

3. *Paragraph 3—Optional Additional Information.* Add more information that credentials you as an excellent candidate, for example, education, certifications, security clearances, languages, availability to travel and/or relocate

4. *Paragraph 4—Conclusion.* Don't get carried away. Make sure to include your contact information and any specifics that will make it easier for them to get in touch with you.

Cover letters do matter, some, but they are not going to make or break your job search. When you get ready to write your cover letter, where do you go first? Your resume? NO! The job posting, specifications, or what you know about the job and the company. Your cover letter must align you with the person the company wants to hire. You want to make a positive and professional first impression and create the kind of impact that will attract interest.

A sample cover letter is included here so you can see how it comes together.

May 10, 2099

Ms. Helen Hunter
Director of Recruiting
Widget, Inc.
1000 Corporate Drive
Big Town, ST 99999

Dear Ms. Hunter:

John Martin, who I worked with at Digital Design Company, suggested I contact you in regard to the Financial Planning and Analysis Manager position at Widget. I know I would be a strong contributor to the company's financial team.

My background and experience make me an excellent fit for this position.

- I have more than 8 years of experience in finance, with 2 managing an FP&A team.
- As a power user of Excel as well as ABC and DEF software, I am effective in an environment where complex financial modeling is the norm.
- I am skilled at building working relationships with business unit executives and staff.
- I have managed high performance teams of up to 6 analysts.

In addition, I have an MBA from Top Dog University and am available to travel as required.

I look forward to talking with you further about this opportunity. My resume is enclosed (or attached). I can best be reached on my cell phone 555-555-5555 or by email at email@email.com.

Sincerely,

*Kelly J. Smart*

Kelly J. Smart

# To Picture or Not to Picture, That Is the Question

CONVENTIONAL WISDOM: No pictures on resumes—it's a legal issue for the hiring organization.

NEW THINKING: Pictures shouldn't be on resumes, but they should be in lots of other places—and they need to be done right.

A dear friend and former colleague was recently nominated for a prestigious award and was soliciting votes. His awesome accomplishments in a challenging technical field, accompanied by a photo, were displayed on the award competition website. One of his supporters and good friends provided him with honest feedback on his photo, which he shared with us.

> *I was glad to vote for you. However, I'm sure you lost lots of votes because of the picture. You look drunk, Neanderthal-jawed, and addle-brained. The shirt might have passed if you had looked intelligent in it, or were just on vacation. But the picture was a bad choice since you are up against guys with PhDs.*

Yikes! While these comments may be a little extreme in their directness, the underlying point is worthy of consideration. People do make decisions based on how you look. And if you don't match up with what they expect, sometimes it undermines your credibility, diminishes your appeal, and creates "noise" in the communication channel.

# Your Professional Presentation

Whenever someone looks you up on LinkedIn, your website, or other online venues, you will be presenting your professional face to the world. Often this is a person's first impression of you. As career coaches who frequently advise people on photographs, we recommend that your photo be appropriate for your audience. Normally, for business professionals, we suggest erring on the side of looking conservatively professional.

For most businessmen, we suggest being photographed in a nice suit and tie, without facial hair and with plain background—you know, "corporate." Yes, we know—facial hair is a personal preference. We simply encourage you to consider what will sell well to your audience. For most businesswomen, we suggest a tailored jacket or sweater with a simple shell underneath, groomed hair and makeup, and jewelry that doesn't distract. If the corporate look isn't suitable, we suggest a business casual look that is appropriate for your profession. There are some exceptions. Highly regarded, widely known people can get away with more casual photos, for the most part. When in doubt, wear what you would wear to an interview, and make sure the photograph projects the professionalism and energy you would want an interviewer to experience.

# Your Photo is Everywhere!

There was a day when resumes routinely contained headshots, especially for executives and aspiring professionals. Then came anti-discrimination laws and the EEOC, and resumes were stripped of photographs to prevent even a hint of non-compliance. Some companies immediately discarded any resumes that contained photos. Although in the United States, most companies don't keep photos in their official Applicant Tracking Systems, that doesn't stop recruiters and managers from wanting to see pictures. Just because your photo isn't on your resume, that doesn't mean it can't be easily found. Thanks to social media, photos are everywhere. Even if recruiters can't officially get to your photo, they can find you through their personal social media accounts. By the way, rules are different outside the U.S.

For many years, corporations have espoused the philosophy that the "user interface" is, in fact, the face of the company. That interface can be a receptionist on the phone, the company's home page on the Internet, the automated systems with which they do business, and even their logo and brand. Applying this principle to you personally, your photo is part of your "brand" and an important interface to your professional world—for job searching and also for doing business. More importantly, your picture provides an opportunity to make a good first impression.

So while putting a picture on your resume is a no-no, you do want your photograph to be found and you want it to represent the brand you intend. The important places for professional photos are LinkedIn, your bio, company or personal websites. In fact, recruiters, hiring executives, and networking contacts frequently go to these places to look at your picture. The photos you post on Facebook, on a dating site, or have professionally taken for your engagement are not good choices. Even some professionally taken pictures, including those taken by corporate photographers who come on executive picture day, may not present you at your best. A bad picture is worse than no picture at all. Take the time to get it right.

## Six Tips for a Great Photo

A professional headshot should be cropped at your upper arms with the focus on your face. It's a *head* shot after all, not a book cover photo. Most are vertically rectangular, but you will need a square format for LinkedIn. Here are some additional guidelines to consider.

1. Headshots can be taken by a professional photographer or by a friend or family member with experience using a camera. Regardless, the adage "a picture is worth a thousand words" applies here. People will make instant judgments about you when they view your headshot.

2.  If the headshot is not done professionally, try to find someone who can "Photoshop" the background to a plain color. For most people, light grey works best. However, beige or light blue may be better for others. For someone familiar with Photoshop, it should only take a few minutes to remove your office, the fireplace mantle, the dog, shrubs, or the door frame from the photo.

3.  Even some professional photos, like those taken for dating sites or your personal celebrations, may not be appropriate for business purposes. Think about your pose ahead of time, and don't rely on the photographer to get it right. To get an idea of what works, check out your colleagues and competitors on LinkedIn and see which ones you think communicate best.

4.  Attire in general: Wear what you would wear to an interview.

5.  Attire for women: Clothing should be tailored and not distracting. Fashion forward is fine. Color is fine—solids are best. Jewelry is fine. Just make sure it doesn't get in the way. Usually a jacket or sweater with or without a shell photograph well. Collars on blouses rarely sit right, don't portray professional stature well, and can easily become dated as styles change. Whatever color, style, or jewelry you wear  should complement your coloring and personal style. Pay attention to your hair and makeup so that it is effective for photography. Makeup can be heavier than everyday wear to bring out your features. You might consider having your hair and makeup professionally done.

6. Attire for men: Standard business attire—suit and tie—is appropriate most of the time. Select colors to complement your coloring and personal style. Err on the side of conservative. Make sure that the collar on your shirt and your tie knot sit perfectly at your neck. If you don't know how to pick out the right clothes or you have difficulty with fit, get guidance at a good men's store. Get a  good professional haircut. Make sure you have shaved recently—no 5 o'clock shadow unless you are a "hunk" applying for modeling or acting gigs.

Ultimately, you want your photo to project the personal power, energy, and enthusiasm that people would want to have in a colleague. The person looking at the photo should feel engaged with you. Your headshot should make the impression that you would want to make in person at an interview. Be prepared and then relax and let the photographer do his or her job.

# What's Wrong with Resumes of Recent Graduates?

CONVENTIONAL WISDOM: Work history is the core of all resumes.

NEW THINKING: Graduates should highlight their education, not their part-time jobs.

New graduate resumes shouldn't look, or even try to look, like the resumes of people with work experience. Why? Unless you plan to have a career in retail, fast food, or filing and copying, employers don't care about most part-time jobs, except to show that you had the energy and work ethic to help fund your education.

When this statement was shared at a conference for journalism students, one young man asked, "What about my work at the book store?" Our response was, "Do you plan to have a career in retail or publishing?" He admitted he did not. "Then, why would you want to highlight your work at the book store on your resume?"

The problem with most new graduate resumes is they try to look like resumes for experienced people with years of work history. The graduate thereby misses out on highlighting their new education and the promise for their future. Employers are primarily interested in a graduate's potential—knowledge, skills, and leadership capabilities. Thus, new grads will want to showcase their education, leadership, and educational achievements rather than part-time employment that normally isn't even relevant to their career choices.

# Five Steps to a Great New Grad Resume

When writing your resume, keep in mind that your resume is being read through the eyes of the recruiter or hiring manager. A good education isn't enough. You have to stand out compared to other candidates who also have a good education. You do this by being specific about your courses, your projects, your leadership activities, and your awards.

1.  Credential yourself as well as your college and the program you were enrolled in. Did you graduate with honors? List your GPA (if it's a good one), your major, and even a sentence or two about the school you attended. For example, if you attended the number one engineering school in the country, show that under the name of the school. Or, your school may not be well known, but the music department is world class. In this case, credential the program. Also include your thesis work, capstone project, internships, and externships.

2.  List relevant courses, about half a dozen. Choose the ones that are really going to make a difference to the people who are going to hire you. For example, if you are applying to work for a human resources department, you may want to list a course on employment law or multicultural leadership.

3.  List organizations that you were a part of. These include honor societies, subject-specific societies (such as the Math Club), student government societies, and social and cultural clubs. Answer the question, *What organizations did I belong to that credential me professionally?*

4. List extracurricular and campus leadership positions under the title of "Leadership," such as "Editor of the School Newspaper," "President of the Debate Club," or "Captain of the Tennis Team."

5. Last but not least, list your in-school work experience. Start with stuff that matters, such as "German Department Teaching Assistant" or "Marketing Assistant," and then include brief information on jobs that aren't relevant to your career.

# Resume Structure for Major Career Change

If you have gone back to school to redirect your career into a significantly different field, you should use this structure for your resume too. Your education should be presented at the beginning of your resume to highlight your new educational credentials, followed by your work experience. In most cases, your work experience will be more important and valuable to the new role compared to an inexperienced new graduate, so this section will be more comprehensive and should still tie to the new direction as much as possible. We also suggest that you list your degrees and schools at the end of the resume because that is where recruiters or computers will be looking for it.

When all is said and done, your resume should highlight what the employer cares about—your potential, the quality of school and educational work, and the competencies you bring to the opportunity.

# Much Ado about Nothing—
## Overused Buzzwords

CONVENTIONAL WISDOM: According to highly publicized sources, resumes and profiles should avoid common buzzwords.

NEW THINKING: Don't overreact to the media hype on buzzwords—use them thoughtfully and strategically.

Recently, LinkedIn released an analysis of 135 million accounts on its network. It identified the 10 most overused buzzwords that people use on their professional profiles.

- ▶ Creative
- ▶ Effective
- ▶ Organizational
- ▶ Extensive Experience
- ▶ Track Record
- ▶ Motivated
- ▶ Innovative
- ▶ Problem Solving
- ▶ Communication Skills
- ▶ Dynamic

These words may be totally different than the words five years or ten years from now, but the general public will likely have the same reaction. They will rush to remove these words from their profiles. The minute they see the word "overused," people immediately assume they shouldn't use them.

We would put this under the category of "much ado about nothing." Overused or not, these words don't matter that much. Recruiters don't search LinkedIn profiles for personal characteristics like "creative" or "dynamic." They search by key functional skills, job titles, companies where employed, and credentials. These should be the focus when building your LinkedIn profile.

There is nothing wrong with using descriptive words. As a matter of fact, descriptive words do have their place, and they can help build "pictures" for the reader of who you are. And the most used words simply reflect the perceived current employment culture.

Quite often, these words will show up in LinkedIn recommendations. That's fine. You want authentic recommendations that "come from the heart." Many recruiters read recommendations for trends. If all your recommendations say you are "creative," you probably are.

There's no need to lose sleep over "overused" word lists and scrub your profile of these commonplace descriptions. Instead, leave them alone and focus on what really matters—effectively presenting your skills, experience, education, and knowledge.

# ABOUT VISIBILITY AND ACCESS:

## NETWORKING

# Networking by the Numbers

CONVENTIONAL WISDOM: Networking is a numbers game. Collect as many business cards as your pockets or purse can hold.

NEW THINKING: Networking is not about quantity, it's about quality.

How many business cards do you typically collect at a "networking" event—5, 20, 50?

It doesn't matter how many people you've collected cards from if you can't remember who they are, or what you are going to do to follow up with them. In many cases where card collecting becomes a contest, the people represented by the cards in your briefcase won't remember you and may have no reason to assist you once you walk out the door. If collecting as many cards as possible is your strategy, you may as well just toss them in a shoebox under your bed.

If, on the other hand, you walk out with the business cards of five people with whom you've really connected and you have a follow-up activity planned for each, you're more likely to convert these contacts into something meaningful and productive.

# Eight Tips for Nailing Your Networking Strategy

Here are some tips for getting to the right people and making it worthwhile.

1.  Choose the right places to network. While career groups can be useful for mutual support, possibly sharing leads, and learning opportunities, the best networking venues are places where hiring managers and senior business leaders are hanging out.

2.  Be prepared with your "ask." Before you set your foot inside the room, have your goals in mind. What do you want to accomplish before you leave? Why did you choose this group for networking? Like just about anything in life and business, if you are crystal clear about what you want to achieve, you'll be far more likely to stay on task and be successful.

3.  Work the room. If you're serious about networking, this is not just a get-out-of-the-office-or-house luncheon or fun cocktail reception. There is someone there you need to know. Scan the setting and choose your target intentionally. Find a polite way to enter the conversation if he or she is already engaged. Don't just stand there smiling and nodding your head. If they are standing or sitting alone, just introduce yourself.

4.  Be discriminating. As soon as possible, evaluate whether the person you are talking to is going to be beneficial to you. Can they help you achieve your goals—tonight (or ever)? If not, politely excuse yourself and move on quickly. Don't waste your valuable time being friendly. Yes, this may sound harsh. But remember, you are on a mission, and you need to get on with it. This is not to suggest that you behave like a self-absorbed, only-in-it-for-me kind of person. Good networking is a balanced give-and-take process. You probably know some people who have a reputation as a "user," and you don't want to be one of them.

5. Establish rapport. Rapport is a powerful mechanism for effective communication. At the very least, find something you have in common, and build on that to get to know them better.

6. Find a reason for follow-up. And do it relatively quickly. Remember, in the quid-pro-quo world of networking, you must always be thinking about WIIFT (what's in it for them). There are many possibilities—almost any of them will do. It may be to share an article or a book you read recently. Best of all is to swap valuable contacts. If you can introduce them to someone they want to meet, then you have the perfect opportunity to get an introduction to someone they know who you want to meet.

7. Move on. Once you have an action plan with one person, move on to another. You should be able to create a meaningful engagement with several people within 30 to 40 minutes. You don't want to get cornered or corner someone else. Keep moving.

8. Follow-up religiously. A component of credibility and character is doing what you say you're going to do. Even if you follow up with a phone call, send an email message too. In your email, you can easily include a restatement about what you are looking for. Be sure to include your professional bio or resume or both.

If you do all those things successfully with four or five people in each networking event, your chances of achieving something valuable and productive are significantly improved—especially compared to the shoebox full of cards.

## The Networking Fab Five

Clients say over and over again, "I don't know very many people." We shouldn't be surprised anymore, but we still find this belief unbelievable. Malarky. In reality, most people actually know hundreds of people and often have over 500 names in their address books.

But for our clients, perception is reality, so we offer this helpful hint. Consider who you know in The Networking Fab Five. There are five categories of professionals who are typically good networkers who have a well above average network of contacts. The reason is that what they do for a living involves getting involved in the community, building strong business relationships, cultivating positive reputations, and staying abreast of who's who in their business and industry. When you network with someone in these professions, you magically have access to a broad wide array of potentially valuable connections. The Fab Five categories are:

- Corporate attorneys
- Commercial and investment bankers
- Commercial real estate brokers and agents
- Large scale management consultants
- Public accountants, primarily with the large firms

A few more categories of well-connected professionals are worth mentioning, but the breadth and scope of their networks may be more limited or more narrowly applicable for your goals:

- Sales professionals—their contacts may not fit the companies or industries you are targeting
- Headhunters and recruiters—they are hired to fill jobs and may not be motivated to help you.
- Residential real estate brokers and agents—they know quite a few people but maybe not the people in hiring positions
- Local CPA firms and financial consultants—same reason

Our bet is that you actually know more people than you think. And if you really think deeply about who you know, you will discover rich networking opportunities that may not have been obvious to you.

# Where the Action Is

**CONVENTIONAL WISDOM**: Job search support groups are good places to network.

**NEW THINKING**: While job search support groups serve an important role for job seekers, there are better places to network.

Job search support groups are just that—support groups. With a few rare exceptions, everyone there is unemployed. Sure, there may be a few generous and open-minded souls who will share leads and point you in the direction of actual job openings, but for the most part, people do not come to these events just to help others. They come to help themselves. It's just fine to join job search support groups for support, but don't expect to find a job there or meet people who will find you a job.

Another reality is that it's rare to meet senior executives at these places. There are a few notable exceptions—for example when the group is specifically tailored to and exclusive to CEOs, CFOs, CIOs, and other "Chiefs"—but entry into these groups is usually "by invitation only." So the people who come to job search support group meetings are typically first-line managers, professionals (technologists, programmers, accountants, sales representatives), and administrative or clerical personnel.

## Benefits of Job Search Support Groups

Of course, job search support groups provide many valuable benefits, namely:

▶ Excellent speakers and discussions of topics that can be helpful in the job search process

▶ Camaraderie and encouragement from others who are in the same boat

▶ Free or inexpensive resources that assist the job seeker

▶ Compassionate and frequently savvy leadership that provides guidance, advice, and valuable direction

▶ An opportunity to practice your personal introduction and networking skills

▶ A reason to get out of the house and away from the computer

If you are an individual with minimal prior job hunting experience and limited financial resources, these support groups may provide an ideal point of entry for your job search activities.

# Find the Action

So where should you be networking? It's simple. All you need to do is go to where the jobs are and where the people who hire people (or people who know people who hire people) are. In other words, go where the real action is. Consider your target industry, target companies, and target jobs. What events are *they* likely to attend? Go there.

> ▸ Find out where and when your industry's trade associations meet.
>
> ▸ Sign up for education programs or relevant functional events, especially if they are free or inexpensive, that would attract your targets and their colleagues.
>
> ▸ If you are targeting small local businesses, consider attending Chamber of Commerce or Rotary meetings.
>
> ▸ Join college alumni organizations, which are among the best places to network. You will immediately have something important in common, and other alumni often have a strong personal motivation for helping "one of their own."
>
> ▸ Choose high visibility civic and community organizations to get involved in. These are excellent places to network because many corporations sponsor their managers' participation.

# Job Fairs—Yea or Nay?

What about job fairs? Our philosophy on job fairs is "Why not?" Companies who have booths at job fairs are looking for candidates. In theory, that should mean they have open positions, and they're hiring. That's good news, right? You can be your best at job fairs in five steps:

1. Check to see if preregistration is required or available. If so, do it before the deadline.
2. Dress appropriately and professionally.
3. Take plenty of business cards and copies of your resume.

4. Get there early so you have time to introduce yourself to the key companies you are targeting.

5. Pick up company literature and business cards of the company representatives in attendance and follow up like crazy.

Now, for the bad news. Job opportunities are most likely to be entry level or technical skills-based. If that doesn't fit your profile, then maybe there's a better way for you to spend your time. If you decide to attend, you can treat it like any other networking event—focus you efforts, develop even a modicum of rapport, and follow up afterward. At least you'll have a starting introduction to a targeted company.

Hopefully it's old news by now that networking is the key to finding a job. Just going to the "right" event is not a silver bullet. You still must have the courage and chutzpah to meet new people, and you must make a good impression when you do.

Too often we hear candidates describe their regular attendance at these job search support groups and job fairs as their sole "networking" activity. That's just not good enough.

# Beyond the Elevator Pitch

> **CONVENTIONAL WISDOM**: A well-prepared 30-second elevator pitch is an essential networking and interviewing tool. Don't leave home without it.
>
> **NEW THINKING**: A polished personal introduction is essential but not sufficient. In many settings it is better to build rapport and engage others in conversation based on thoughtfully prepared information and messages than to deliver speeches.

The "30-second elevator pitch" is no longer sophisticated enough for most professionals and executives. A whole new level is needed now. A "situational introduction" is your personal pitch specifically based on who you are talking to, taking into consideration what message or messages you want to deliver to that person and how much time is available.

Rather than viewing an introduction as something to be memorized or read from a teleprompter, consider the information about you that can be chosen from a basket or database of material to create and deliver a targeted introduction. As you get comfortable with talking about yourself, it will be easy for you to "reach in" and get what you need for any particular situation.

For example, if you are at a professional luncheon meeting, you may get only 4 to 6 words and five seconds as attendees around the table introduce themselves. At a networking gathering, you may get 15 - 20 seconds. At an interview, you may get a lot longer. Perspectives and agendas will vary depending upon who you are talking with, as well as what you want to focus on—what you do, who you are, what you know.

A situational introduction provides not only a better introduction but also the freedom to relax and let the conversation flow appropriately.

# Social Media Silver Bullet

CONVENTIONAL WISDOM: Using any and every bit of social media you can is smart for your job search.

NEW THINKING: Social media is an essential component of your job search but must be used strategically and carefully.

There are an increasing number of social media sites, but the big three are Facebook, Twitter, and Linkedin. For the most part, social media is ubiquitous and poorly leveraged. Too many people waste time on social media, drain their energy, and achieve mediocre or poor results. Even worse, they can do more harm than good in some of these settings.

The first issue for job seekers is how their online presence is affecting their desirability and personal "brand." Social media is a semi-public forum. Just consider how much of the chatter is meaningless drivel going into the public domain—status updates that nobody cares about, scores from games played, and idiotic tweets. Some people go beyond stupid by posting inappropriate pictures, adding vulgar comments, and participating in lewd conversations. Even if this is presumably among "friends," doesn't anyone realize that this could easily become visible to the public and a potential hiring manager?

Assuming you pay attention to how you "show up" on Facebook and Twitter, are these venues good job hunting grounds? Not really. For now, companies are dabbling in Facebook and Twitter as a means to create customer engagement, branding, and market awareness. And though some employers are "trolling" for prospective employees on Facebook, it's often viewed as creepy and intrusive.

The King Kong of social media for job search and professional networking is LinkedIn. LinkedIn is as close to a career "silver bullet" as you will find. They have several hundred million members, more than half of whom are in the United States, and they are growing by two members per second. One in four members is online every day. It's the go-to site for recruiters and companies looking for talent. It's even putting the job boards out of business. In a recent survey by Jobvite, 93% of job recruiters tap into LinkedIn to find qualified candidates.

## Ten Tips for Using LinkedIn

A successful career management or comprehensive, sophisticated job search strategy will incorporate  LinkedIn. There is a growing pool of resources available—articles, books, webinars, seminars, blogs, in-person classes, speakers, and professional profile consultants— that can provide guidance if you are a LinkedIn novice.

Here are ten tips for using LinkedIn more effectively, in your job search and for business in general:

1.  Starting right now and on a regular basis, spend time beefing up and maintaining your LinkedIn profile. Constantly expand your list of capabilities and features that make your profile a portfolio and a rich source of information for recruiters. We do recommend that while you are making changes and updates to your LinkedIn profile, turn OFF the "notifications" in your profile settings.

2.  Create a targeted, keyword-rich profile. Unlike a classic resume, more is better and provides more visibility and more opportunities for being found in a search. Fill in every single section. You won't be penalized if you're redundant.

3.  Rename your URL to something simpler than the one assigned automatically. We recommend adding your customized URL to your email signature, resume, and business card. It can serve as a personal website.

4.  Upload a suitable picture preferably in the shape of the prescribed format to avoid undesirable automatic cropping. Having an appropriate picture is essential and creates a higher degree of credibility. There is overwhelming evidence that profiles with pictures are more credible than those without.

5.  LinkedIn is also one of the best places to network and find connections to jobs. According to a Nielsen study, the average number of connections for LinkedIn members is around 60 people. The generally accepted number of a stable social network is around 150. However, be careful accepting invitations from people who are in competition to have the largest number of connections possible. Connections are not airline miles. We think it's wise to follow LinkedIn's guidance to accept only connections you actually know or have a legitimate reason for connecting with.

6.  Recruiters are also looking to build networks, so connect with them too.

7.  Solicit recommendations and endorsements and give them in return. Recommendations in particular are a great way to make your fans' comments available in a public forum. Over time, you are creating a portfolio of references that will survive the ebbs and flows of relationships. These will eventually replace those dog-eared hard copy letters of recommendation that in many cases you wrote and they signed.

8.  Join groups—the more the merrier. In particular, you really should be a member of all of the key groups in your industry or function. Alumni groups are also a rich source of networking contacts.

9.  Use your Contact Settings and Opportunity Preferences strategically. If you are employed, you probably don't want to list "career opportunities."

10. Finally, leverage your profile by posting meaningful status updates from time to time that enhance your brand and increase your visibility. Share relevant or poignant articles with your observations or insight. Add comments to other people's posts. Participate in your Groups' Discussions. This is an especially good venue to establish yourself as a subject matter expert.

All of these things enhance your LinkedIn profile and will help you get closer to your dream job.

It takes time and effort to create a top-notch LinkedIn profile. LinkedIn's structure is somewhat rigid and can be a moving target. Especially if you have a complex or unusual job history or if you are technology-challenged, it might be a bit intimidating or overwhelming. Perhaps consider hiring a professional to help develop your profile and teach you how to maintain it.

Social media in career management and job search is here to stay. From now on, you have to be a savvy user of these tools and cognizant that you are more transparent than ever. Be wary, be wise.

## Sample Scripts for LinkedIn Invitations

Think about how you feel when you receive the boilerplate LinkedIn invitation, "I'd like to add you to my professional network on LinkedIn." It comes across as lazy or indifferent. We recommend that you try to personalize every LinkedIn invitation you send out. If you remind your contact how you know them or explain your reasons for connecting, your results will be better.

The most frequent question we run into is, "What should I say?" So here are a few sample invitations to use as a guide in creating your own approach that shows professionalism and personality. Ending your invitation with a question provides a catalyst for further dialogue. You have only 300 characters with spaces to work with—use them wisely.

□ □ □

Hi, [Contact Name]:

Just came across your profile and wanted to add you to my network. I've never been a good networker but have decided to finally get more serious about my LinkedIn connections. It would be helpful to have your phone # and address for my records.

[Your name]
333-444-5555
*[288 characters]*

□ □ □

Hi, [Contact Name]:

I don't know if you remember me, but we met/worked together [when/where]. I ran across your profile on LinkedIn and would like to reconnect. Hope you are doing well.

By the way, how did that [project or event] go?

[Your name]
333-444-5555
*[257 characters]*

□ □ □

Hi, [Contact Name]:

We haven't met personally, but my friend/colleague, [Name of Connection], recommended that I reach out to you. I have an interest and background in big box retail management [or whatever you have in common], so I'd love to connect with you.

When would you be free for a call?

[Your name]
333-444-5555
*[286 characters]*

□ □ □

Hi, [Contact Name]:

I can't believe we haven't connected on LinkedIn yet! Hopefully we'll have time to reconnect and catch up soon. When would you be free for a call or a quick cup of coffee?

[Your name]
333-444-5555
*[216 characters]*

# Beyond Performance and Politics: Visibility Matters

CONVENTIONAL WISDOM: Just do a good job and the company will reward you.

NEW THINKING: Politics, performance, and visibility all play important roles in your career success.

Let's build a pyramid.

*First Level—Performance.* At the first or entry level, you do your job, keep your head down, and perform like a star. This is how you get recognized and promoted early in your career, but it's not a complete, long-term career strategy. At this stage, your personal success will be based 80% on your job performance and 20% on relationships.

*Second Level—Politics.* At this level, you must develop political awareness and become skilled in working with the complex dynamics of relationships and agendas. Your job won't be solely based on politics, but from just beyond entry level through middle management, you should have a pretty good handle on it. Getting a pay raise or promotion is based about 60% on job performance and 40% on politics.

*Third Level—Visibility.* Usually beginning at the director level, you must shift from becoming just a company player to being an industry player. Your goal should be to develop visibility and relationships outside of your department and functional area and also gain visibility outside your company. Pick your head up off your desk and get out of your office. At this point and for the rest of your career, politics and visibility play crucial roles in your advancement and success.

# Be Visible Earlier Rather Than Later

Excellent performance is always a factor. In fact, the higher you go in an organization, the more performance and competency is taken for granted. You wouldn't normally be concerned about whether the CFO knows debits and credits—it's assumed. The differentiating factors have to do with navigating the company's political landscape and being well connected with and respected by people outside your immediate domain and beyond your company. Even at the very early stages of your career, it is helpful to begin to build these relationships and to hone your political savvy.

There are several ways to cultivate visibility. Because these activities are typically beneficial to your company, there are ways to get involved with its full support and blessing. Here are some possibilities.

- ▸ Volunteer to participate or lead a cross-functional company project or task force.

- ▸ Get involved in a special interest group or community activity sponsored by the company.

- ▸ Join organizations, participate fully, and consider becoming one of the leaders of those organizations.

- ▸ Network with others by joining committees, working at conferences, and representing your organization at industry events.

- ▸ Position yourself as an expert or authority by leading a workshop, writing for a publication, authoring a book, teaching a seminar, or speaking at a conference.

- ▸ Become involved with industry events, national roundtables, or university think tanks.

- ▸ Volunteer to become a source for the press. This can increase your chances of being quoted in trade publications, industry newsletters, and general business press. Be sure to check your company policies.

## How Visible Are You?

In addition to cultivating your personal visibility, the most successful professionals ensure that they can be easily found by recruiters and other interested parties. Where they are looking, you want to be found. LinkedIn is number #1, by a long shot. You might also do a Google search on your name and a key characteristic, and see what comes up. If you are not even on the first 10 pages, you have quite a lot of work to do.

# Fallacy of Job Boards

**CONVENTIONAL WISDOM:** Job boards makes job searching easier.

**NEW THINKING:** Job boards are designed to help companies find employees, not to help job seekers find jobs.

For the uninitiated, job boards like Monster.com seem like great places to find and apply for jobs. What people don't realize is how the odds are stacked against them. No matter how qualified—no matter how much of a perfect fit—your chances of being considered for a job from these boards are slim.

## Job Boards Explained

There are many different types of job boards:

- Large all-purpose career boards, like Monster.com and The Ladders
- Company website careers pages
- Consolidators, like Indeed.com, that have no new information but crawl the Internet and pull together into one place all the jobs that are posted
- Specialty boards such as for hospitality or healthcare jobs, that are industry or function specific, many of which are maintained by professional associations

Job boards are designed for companies and recruiters to make data collection easier and to attract lots of job candidates. Whether you apply for a job on an Internet job board or company website, applications and resumes go into database pools that can be searched based on specific parameters, key words, or attributes that, in the recruiters' opinions, best match the job requirements.

The good news is that job boards are an opportunity to gain a remarkable amount of market intelligence and a place to find jobs you may not have known about. Once a job opportunity has been identified, you should apply for the job online and then intensify and focus your networking on getting your foot in the door.

## Odds Are Slim

While job boards make market research easier, they don't provide any assurance of a meaningful process for being selected for an interview, regardless of qualifications. The odds of actually being found from a job board are remarkably slim.

It would seem that a job board is a logical place to find a job opportunity and apply for it. Many job seekers spend hours searching these postings, find their "perfect job", fill out the endless forms, push the "apply" button, and then expect the company to contact them to schedule the interview. "Abracadabra" they're on their way to a fabulous job.

But the reality is that hundreds or thousands of people are also applying. Each person is a single speck in the universe of job seekers.

Furthermore, the employer is interested in finding just a few well-qualified applicants for the job. Lots and lots of candidates are good, and when they find their quota, they stop looking. They are not in the business of interviewing more candidates than are necessary to fill the job.

The point is that applying for jobs on job boards is like playing Black Jack in Vegas. The odds of beating the house are slim, but understanding how the game is played can improve your success. So, make the best use of applying for jobs in this medium, understand the basic rules, do the best you can, don't agonize, and get on with the real work of your job search—networking.

Of course, some people have found jobs directly from job boards, but statistically speaking, the probabilities are not in your favor.

# Real Job, Fake Job

**CONVENTIONAL WISDOM:** There are a lot of jobs I can apply for on the Internet.

**NEW THINKING:** There are a lot of jobs you can apply for on the Internet, but many of these jobs are non-existent, inactive, or obsolete.

For sure, some people have found jobs on the Internet. In many of those cases, other steps such as networking and persistent self-marketing played an integral role in landing those jobs.

In reality, while there are certainly real jobs on the Internet, there are an amazing number of jobs there that are either "fake" or no longer viable. If your primary job search strategy is to apply for jobs you find on the Internet, you are going to be waiting a long time for the phone to ring—if it ever does.

One of our clients with a prestigious college degree came to us after applying for over 100 jobs on the Internet. He was increasingly frustrated not having gotten any responses, phone calls, or emails, other than one or two rejections. This is the quintessential example of the inadequacy of Internet job search.

# The Reality of Internet Jobs

Jobs posted on job boards or company websites typically fall into one of three categories: 1) Real jobs, 2) Fishing jobs; and 3) Mistake jobs.

*Real jobs.* These are jobs that really exist, and companies are willing to screen through the hundreds, even thousands, of responses to find the right candidate. Unfortunately, if you don't match all of the required specs—every single one—and most of the preferred ones, you are not going to make the cut. You have a better chance of winning a jackpot at the slot machine.

*Fishing jobs.* These jobs also fall into three categories. *Contingency fishing* occurs when recruiting firms post fake jobs in order to keep their databases fresh. They need readily available candidates for quick responses on recruiting engagements. *Commission fishing* is a tactic used by companies that pay strictly on commission for such pursuits at insurance sales, multilevel marketing, real estate investing, and some full-blown scams. They are usually looking for independent contractors who are interested in sales and marketing. Finally, there are the *No-Way fishing* jobs. These jobs usually already have viable internal or external candidates  in the running, but the company posts them anyway for legal compliance. The companies aren't actually looking for good candidates. They are merely going through the motions, up to and including bringing people in for interviews.

*Mistake jobs.* These jobs might have been real at some point, until company mergers, outsourcing, or hiring freezes cause either a change or cancellation of the original job. Or, the job is simply filled and no longer available. In many cases, it's just easier for the company to let the original posting expire than to go in and change it or cancel it. The result is numerous listings for jobs that no longer exist.

It may be impossible for you to differentiate between real and fake jobs on the Internet. So we tell our clients that it's fine to apply for Internet jobs. However, if they are spending more than 5-10% of their job search time in these pursuits, then they need to refocus their efforts on more productive activities, like serious networking.

# The World According to Recruiters

> **CONVENTIONAL WISDOM:** Recruiters will help and support my job search efforts.
>
> **NEW THINKING:** Recruiters work for the folks that pay the bill—and you will be more successful in getting the attention you need if you understand their business model.

Otherwise savvy business people are frequently confused or angered by their experiences with recruiters. In large part, this is because they have not looked closely at the recruiting industry's basic business and compensation models. Since this is a business relationship, the path to enlightenment can be found by simply following the money.

The Usual Complaints

- ▶ Recruiters won't call me back.
- ▶ Recruiters won't give me a few minutes of advice on my resume or job search.
- ▶ The recruiters I know never seem to have a job opportunity for me.
- ▶ Recruiters won't consider me for a search even though I know I am perfectly qualified.
- ▶ If I do network my way into a company, I end up talking with the recruiter anyway.

> ▶ If the recruiter didn't "find" me, I don't get fair consideration.
> ▶ After I've been interviewed, a recruiter may be attentive and then suddenly disappear.
> ▶ They string me along and keep me hanging.

None of this seems rational or fair, and certainly not considerate. Understanding how the recruiting world works and how recruiters make their money goes a long way to helping you have a more productive and less frustrating experience. If you understand their perspective, you have an opportunity to work with recruiters effectively, positively, and to your mutual benefit. It is a dance, and you can be a good partner.

## Why Won't They Talk to Me?

Recruiters work for their clients, and the clients pay the bill. Regardless of the type of firm, recruiters ultimately get paid for executing successful searches by delivering qualified and interested candidates. If you are not a match for an active search, every minute a recruiter spends with you is a minute that he or she is not making money. Unless you are a valuable resource for the future, recruiters tend not to extend common courtesies such as returning phone calls.

## Why Don't They Have a Job For Me?

Surprise! External recruiters control only 10-15% of the job market. An individual recruiter conducts only a small number of assignments each year, often as few as 8 to 10 for executive positions. Those searches span positions and sometimes industries and geographies as well. Recruiters are tied tightly to a job specification, and more tightly in a buyer's economy. The company is looking for candidates that "fit" the spec, not "out-of-the-box" talent. The odds that any individual recruiter is working on a search that is a perfect fit for you at the time you are looking for a new opportunity is infinitesimally small.

# Why Aren't They Interested In Me?

Good recruiters learn what their clients want to fill the position. In addition to the job description, the recruiter usually understands the company culture, the history of incumbents in the position, and the private or unstated criteria on which the company will ultimately make a decision. The recruiter needs to find candidates that not only can do the job, but who also can be "sold" to the client.

Clients pay a lot of money for recruiting services—sometimes as much as 35% of first year compensation. And the higher the position, the more likely the client pays travel expenses for the recruiter to conduct interviews. CATCH 22: The client is paying dearly for recruiting services, so the client will funnel all candidates through the recruiter for evaluation in order to get the full benefit of those services. On the other hand, recruiters need clients to value their investment; therefore, recruiters have a vested interest in "finding" the candidate. If the client finds the successful candidate rather than the recruiter, it can affect the perceived value of the services.

# Why Do They String Me Along?

Recruiting assignments often have erratic paths. They start quickly, go on hold, change requirements, change hiring executive, or even get cancelled altogether. The recruiter is required to go with the client's flow and, at the same time, maintain an inventory of ready prospects. Furthermore, the recruiter never truly knows what the client or other candidates are going to do. He or she always needs a pipeline until an offer has been made and accepted, and sometimes even until the person actually starts the job.

# What Do I Do About It?

Recruiters are still an important channel in any job search. It is important to stay on their radar screens because no one ever knows when a great opportunity will suddenly surface, or which recruiter will have it. At the most senior levels, executive search firms are universally used when companies go to the external market to fill a position. Such a search is complex and time consuming. It requires extraordinary skills and is often confidential. Search firms must have or be able to get access to the right people. Clients use recruiters for finding managers and staff so they can outsource tasks to skilled professionals.

By understanding how recruiters work, you can position yourself to get the benefit of this channel.

- ▸ *Do* network with the appropriate people and get to know recruiters in your field.
- ▸ *Offer* to be a source and provide quality referrals.
- ▸ *Do* keep your resume up-to-date and in their hands or databases.
- ▸ *Do not* expect anything in return.
- ▸ *Do not* take recruiter behavior personally.
- ▸ *Do* be connected and visible. Recruiters have all kinds of tools for finding you. Make sure you can be found!

## Who's Who in Recruiting

There is a lot of confusion about the recruiting industry. Not all recruiters are created equal or follow the same revenue structure. Some get paid for doing the work and others get paid for getting a candidate hired. A firm may be involved in more than one type of recruiting services.

Here is a guide to the most common types of recruiters.

- **Retained.** Recruiters that are "retained" are like consultants. Most call themselves Retained Executive Search Consultants. They get paid for each engagement, regardless of whether their candidate gets hired or even if anyone gets hired. For obvious reasons, these are exclusive assignments—no other firm is representing the same job at the same time. They have deep motivation to do a good job so that the company will continue to use their services over the long run. Because of the cost and the exclusivity, they represent positions at the high-income executive level, but not always.

  In some cases, recruiters will provide a hybrid type of engagement such that they will get paid for their work in installments, but with the last payment contingent on a final placement of their candidate.

- **Contingency.** Contingency recruiters typically work at the professional and middle management levels. They get paid only when their candidates get hired, regardless of the amount of work that they do. They may or may not be engaged exclusively by the company. Some contingency recruiters market good candidates to companies where they have a relationship in the hopes that the company might hire the person and they would get paid for the placement. Often when the economy weakens, there are more recruiters who try to expand their revenue by "finding jobs" for individuals.

- **Staffing.** Staffing is a widespread pillar of talent acquisition. Staffing agencies handle a variety of temporary, temp-to-perm, and full-time positions focused on clerical, administrative, technical, and operational jobs. It is used in every profession and industry and is often the platform for spot hiring and staff augmentation. They typically get paid fees based on hours worked or a placement fee.

- **In-house.** Large companies maintain internal recruiting personnel whose responsibilities range from full service recruiting for all levels of employees and executives to managing contracts with outside recruiters. The sophistication of Internet and recruiting technologies provide broader and more efficient access to the market for internal recruiters than ever before.

# Too Much of a Good Thing?

---

**CONVENTIONAL WISDOM:** Any PR is good PR.

**NEW THINKING:** Too much visibility can be "noise" in the system and is not necessarily a good thing.

---

We've heard this for a long time, haven't we? Any PR is good PR. It's based on the notion that public relations is all about managing the reputation, communication and recognition of a company, a product or a brand. If the goal is to create a "top of mind" status for something, then getting a lot of publicity can achieve that, even if it's "bad" publicity.

People generally agree these days that getting a ton of bad PR can actually damage a brand or a reputation rather than help it. These situations leave a sour taste in our mouths. Warren Buffett said, "It takes twenty years to build a reputation and five minutes to ruin it. If you think about that, you'll do things differently."

## Check Yourself Out

Hopefully you are not under indictment or being investigated. You are, we hope, cultivating your visibility and gathering good publicity as part of your job search and career development strategy. Let's just check.

- ▶ When you Google your name, what comes up?
- ▶ How many connections do you have on LinkedIn?
- ▶ Do you even have a complete LinkedIn Profile?
- ▶ What have you posted on Twitter lately?
- ▶ When was the last time you added a thoughtful editorial comment on an article of significance?

These are some useful ways to build your visibility using social media resources. And having strong visibility so that you are easily found is a critical ingredient for successful career management. But how much is too much?

# Too Little or Too Much?

There's a fine line between enough and too much. It's probably fair to say that most people err on the side of not doing enough. We are frequently shocked and amazed when a business person tells us they don't even have a LinkedIn profile, let alone have an informational YouTube video posted.

On the other hand, if you are constantly "out there" you run the risk of creating too much "noise." Your message may become diluted, causing confusion about your brand or even creating a negative impression. Further, with quasi-public social media venues like Facebook, even your personal life, family, friends, and social activities can affect your image. Any of your Facebook friends can tag a picture of you, and it might not be one that you would want your boss to see.

Twitter has also become a popular PR tool. Sometimes tweets provide interesting topical tidbits and links to new content on the web. However, some tweets make you think the sender is nuts, obnoxious, or just self-absorbed—not a good impression.

In general, you want to be found by the people who are looking for someone like you. Thus, you have to show up in the places they are looking and make it easy for them to connect with you. Whether it is promoting your business or finding a job or being on an industry's radar screen, it is worthwhile to do some strategic thinking and take some targeted actions. This is not just being on Facebook or Twitter or LinkedIn—or having a website or writing a book. It is knowing what resources are out there and how to use them best for your purposes and investing your time and money selectively and wisely. Then, when opportunity is ready to knock, it can find your door.

The moral of the story is this. More PR is better than less, and getting publicity is a key ingredient in the secret sauce of successful career development. While most of us will agree that any PR is not necessarily good PR, no PR whatsoever is detrimental to establishing and maintaining our personal brands and correspondingly our careers. So we encourage you to focus your efforts on meaningful social media activities. But be very careful that you don't go overboard and become a nuisance.

# ABOUT SALES:

# INTERVIEWING

# Interviewers Know What They Are Doing—or Do They?

CONVENTIONAL WISDOM: Interviewers know how to conduct interviews and can be relied on to obtain the information that supports solid hiring decisions.

NEW THINKING: Interviewer skills span a wide range, and no one, from the hiring company to the prospective employee, should take interviewer competence for granted.

Not too long ago, Businessweek reported that the "standard interview"—the sit-down affair with management or human resources—was only 7% accurate in identifying qualified candidates. Even the more sophisticated assessment centers and situational interviews achieved only 44% and 54% accuracy, respectively. Obviously some of the issue here is with the limitations of the process not just the competence of the interviewer.

However, of all the people who do interviews—from contact center screeners to recruiters (internal and external), to hiring managers and executives to ancillary interviewers such as peers and customers—few are actually trained to interview. Moreover, some interviews take place with randomly selected, unprepared people who occasionally don't even see a resume before they sit down with an applicant.

Consider this scenario. A candidate is scheduled to interview with someone directly involved with the job he has applied for. The person originally scheduled to do the interview is called into an emergency meeting. Because it's too late to reschedule, the original interviewer looks around to see who is available. Seeing that Sally hasn't gone to lunch yet, the interviewer says, "Sally, I have a candidate interview in a few minutes, and I've just been called into an urgent meeting. I'd appreciate your handling this for me," and heads out the door.

How often does this happen? It happens more than you think.

## Control the Interview

Even if you are interviewed by the correct person, there's no guarantee you'll get a good interviewer. Often HR recruiters have had training, but in some cases interviewing is not their core competency. Many have learned by trial and error. Surprisingly, this also holds true for a lot of external recruiters. In the case of hiring managers, their jobs are to run their departments—and interviewing is only an occasional function. Managers may not be good at interviewing or even like it and are rarely professionally trained. Worst of all some poor interviewers think they are really good at it.

As a job candidate, getting a good interviewer is a random occurrence. You just never know. But don't throw your hands up in despair quite yet. If you understand the structure and process of interviewing, you can relax, help guide the event, and influence the outcome—even if the interviewer has no skills whatsoever. For example, if you understand the ideal model for the process that should guide the person on the other side of a transaction, then you will be more successful in achieving your desired outcome. With this level of understanding, you will be better prepared to respond to questions and capitalize on the situation, no matter how disjointed or unprepared the interviewer is.

# Understanding Types of Interviews

Not all interviews are created equal. There is a natural flow, and each type of interview has a specific objective. Sometimes these will be combined and may be repeated more than once, but the objectives remain constant. With the flow in mind, you can keep track of where you are and handle yourself appropriately.

Below is a simple schematic of the typical interview flow.

| Types of Interviews | Interviewer's Objective |
| --- | --- |
| First Contact | General fit, interest? Get paperwork. |
| Screen | Invest time in this candidate? |
| Comprehensive (usually the Boss) | Give serious consideration to this candidate? |
| Peer Team | Input (not decision makers) |
| Boss's Peers/Customers | Input (not decision makers) |
| Boss's Boss | Veto, often finalist only |
| Informal Social (top executives only) | Chemistry |
| Board of Directors (top executives only) | Affirmation, veto or courtesy, usually finalist only |

# Understanding the Interview Process

For telephone, video, and sit-down interviews, there is a model that can be considered the "ideal" interview. Since this is a theoretical construct, most interviewers do not follow it in sequence. However, with this model in mind, a candidate can understand what a question is about and construct a properly targeted answer.

- ▸ *The First 5 Minutes:* This is designed to establish the candidate's high-level qualifications (interest, compensation, availability), test basic capabilities, and identify the basis for a chemistry match.

- ▸ *Alignment with Spec:* This is designed to determine the match between the candidate's "resume" and the position requirements, determine the candidate's domain knowledge, and evaluate the candidate's capabilities and potential contribution to the company.

- ▸ *Conducting Business:* Here the interviewer finds out the type of environment the candidate is most comfortable in, the type of people the candidate likes to work with, and the candidate's management style.

- ▸ *Communication and Perspective:* This explores how other people view the candidate and how the candidate views him/herself, others, and organizations.

- ▸ *Career and Life Management:* This identifies the candidate's career goals and evaluates the candidate's career management skills.

- ▸ *Tough, Unexpected Questions:* These questions are designed to test the candidate's flexibility, quick thinking, and ability to be articulate under pressure.

This information may be gathered in a single interview, over several interviews, or even repeated from interview to interview. Some interviewers may be asked to focus on a specific area. With this model as a compass, candidates being interviewed can continuously maintain their bearings.

# Demystifying Behavioral Interviews

> **CONVENTIONAL WISDOM:** Behavioral interviews are tricky and are designed to stump you.
>
> **NEW THINKING:** If you understand how a behavioral interview works, it's a piece of cake.

If you're in the process of interviewing, it's likely you'll hear the term "behavioral interview," and you may not know what it means. However, there's a good chance that even if you don't know what the term means, you have experienced a behavioral interview.

# Predicting the Future from the Past

A "behavioral interview" is designed to examine a candidate's past behaviors. It's based on the assumption that past behavior is the best predictor of future performance.

Behavioral interviews are popular today. They are used at some point in nearly every interviewing process, even if the interviewer is not particularly skilled at the method.

# Recognizing the Behavioral Interview

How do you recognize the behavioral interview? In a behavioral interview, you will be asked to describe a time when you did something that exemplified a particular characteristic, quality, or competency that the interviewer is interested in. Most behavior interview questions start with, "Tell me about a time when. . ." or "Give me an example of a situation when. . . ."

An interviewer may stop after you give your answer. However, a skilled interviewer will use your answer as a jumping off point to explore your actions and rationale more fully. It becomes a dance. Since the interviewer doesn't have your answer in advance, a truly good interviewer will be able to move from the first question to the next and the next, spontaneously drilling down into your experience based on the information you are providing. The flow of the questions will be focused on determining if you have the competencies—knowledge, skills, and abilities—needed to do the job well. The process is not just a random exploration of your past.

For example, you might be asked, "Tell me about a time when you had to make a critical decision in your boss' absence." Depending on what you say, the next question might be, "How could you have handled that situation differently?" or "How would you handle the same situation differently in the future?" Or, it might be "How did your boss evaluate your decision?" or "What kinds of outside influences affected the outcome of your actions?"

# Behavior Interview Prep

What can you do to prepare for a behavioral interview?

While there's no way to prepare for the specific questions you will be asked, you can prepare yourself for this kind of question in general.

1.  Select stories about your experiences that are relevant to your targeted job.
2.  Prepare your scenario using the SAR model:
    a.  Specific situation
    b.  Actions your took
    c.  Results—what happened

It's important to keep in mind that it is not a matter of right or wrong answers. Also, don't get rattled if some interviewers take the process to the extreme. For example, one candidate reported that his interviewers had each been assigned a specific set of behavioral interview questions that they were required to rigidly ask. They robotically asked the questions assigned and made no attempt to build rapport. They did not engage in any exploration, conversation, or dialogue. While it made for an unpleasant experience, the candidate was well-prepared and just took it in stride.

Remember, this type of interviewing is a dance in which the interviewer starts off but then follows your lead. Understanding how behavioral interviews work and having your thoughtfully developed scenarios to draw on, you can relax and go with the flow.

# Interviewers Don't Have "The List"

CONVENTIONAL WISDOM: Interviewers frequently ask you to describe your best (or worst) example of a skill, attribute, or experience, and you need to have the top item ready to go.

NEW THINKING: It doesn't matter what the best (or worst) situation or example really is. What matters is that your answer is aligned well with the requirements, challenges, and responsibilities of the job for which you are interviewing.

Some of the most common interview questions, especially by interviewers who believe past behavior is the best predictor of future performance, begin with "Tell me about . . ." These questions often include superlatives like "least," "most," "best," and "worst."

- What is the **least** successful project you have managed?
- What is the **most** difficult personnel situation you have ever handled?
- What are you **most** proud of in your career?
- What do you consider your **greatest** strength/weakness?
- What is the **best** company culture you have worked in?
- What is the **hardest** decision you have made?
- What is the **most** complex customer relationship you have dealt with?

If you have ever been on the receiving end of one of these questions—and you most likely have—you've probably felt that you had the double duty of (a) scanning your brain for an event that fits the superlative and (b) crafting a good answer.

Almost always, candidates sort through their experiences, retrieve relevant situations, and mentally rank the list in order of "most," "least," etc. using their own evaluation criteria. They automatically believe they must select the perfect "top" example in order to answer the question "right." Unfortunately, candidates often choose to talk about a situation or attribute that may not align well with the requirements, challenges, and responsibilities of the job they are interviewing for.

Guess what? Interviewers have no access to your list of experiences. They have no idea if the example chosen is in fact the "best" or ranks somewhere in the middle of the pack.

## The Best Answer Isn't the "Best" (or "Worst") Answer

In answering this type of question, alignment is the key. Remember, these "behavioral interviewing questions" are designed to determine your future performance based on past behavior. Once you have selected your answer to the question, you will want to construct your response using SAR (Situation, Actions, Results) or a similar model.

This is not a test. By understanding that no one has "The List" but you, you won't be graded on getting #1 right, but rather on having an example that is a great fit with the job you are interviewing for.

# The Three Bears: Too Long, Too Short, Just Right

> **CONVENTIONAL WISDOM:** The correct length for an interview answer is intuitive.
>
> **NEW THINKING:** Calibrating the amount of time spent answering a question is important for keeping the interviewer engaged with you, as well as for keeping your answer on track. There is a method for getting it right.

**M**ost people have no idea how long the answer to an interview question should be. When an individual is verbose, the interviewer quickly loses interest or stops listening entirely. Alternatively, some people don't provide enough information, and the interviewer has to ask (if they bother) a series of questions to get the answer they really want from the candidate.

The following approach helps an individual calibrate the right amount of time and answer questions clearly and succinctly. The approach will also help candidates when a question throws them off guard.

# Three Steps to Good Answers

1. Restate the question.
2. Answer the question in one sentence or less. Don't hold it for the surprise ending.
3. Explain the answer or give a reason or example in a couple of sentences.

Here are some examples of how the "Three Bears" would answer an interview question. The first answer is too long, while the second is too short. The third answer is—you guessed it—just right.

**Q**: How quickly do you learn new technology?

**Papa Bear**: I'm always around new things and have lots of experience with it. I'm pretty good at learning stuff, and I love technology in general. There was this one time when I was at a check processing company, and we got all this new equipment in. They didn't give us any training, and so we had to learn everything ourselves. My boss only gave us one week to learn it. We couldn't find the manuals for about the first week, then we had to . . . blah, blah, blah, blah, blah. . . . *(too long, unfocused, boring)*.

**Mama Bear:** Very fast, it's easy for me *(too short, lacks valuable information, doesn't sell candidate well)*.

**Baby Bear:** I learn new technology very quickly. I work in a fast-paced company where we have to be up to date on their systems, which change frequently. Since we usually don't get a lot of training before we start using the new systems, I have become very proficient at learning what I need to know from manuals and hands-on experience *(just right)*.

With a little attention and practice, you can answer interview questions "just right."

# Good Interviews Are More Than Q&A Exercises

CONVENTIONAL WISDOM: Interviews consist of the interviewer asking you questions, which you answer professionally and articulately. Then, you ask the interviewer a few thoughtful, salient questions that underscore your preparation for the interview and interest in the job.

NEW THINKING: The best interviews—those that really get to the heart of the matter—evolve organically into a back-and-forth discussion between you and the interviewer.

Typical interviews tend to be Q&A sessions. They don't have to be, and the best ones aren't. Most people—both those being interviewed and those doing the interviewing—believe that interviews should follow a certain structure. For the first 85% of the time allotted, the interviewer asks the questions and the interviewee answers. The last 15% are usually devoted to the interviewee asking some questions about the company or job that demonstrate interest and preparation.

It is possible to display your background, skills, experience, and knowledge, as well as to indicate how you would handle yourself on the job, using this method. Unfortunately, it does nothing to create rapport. This bland approach will limit your ability to align yourself with the company's needs and may even prevent you from getting the crucial information you need about the job.

# The Five-Star Interview Model

The best interviews should be a dialogue between you and the interviewer. The secret is using our "Five-Star Interview Model."

| | |
|---|---|
| ★ | Their Question |
| ★ ★ | Your Answer |
| ★ ★ ★ | Your Question |
| ★ ★ ★ ★ | Their Answer |
| ★ ★ ★ ★ ★ | Your Alignment Response |

For example:

★ **Interviewer:** How do you monitor performance in your organization?

★ ★ **You:** I rely heavily on feedback that I get from customers and key people inside our company.

★ ★ ★ **You:** Are there performance issues in the group that will need immediate attention?

★ ★ ★ ★ **Interviewer:** This group has only been together a short time and, frankly, I don't yet have a good assessment of how they are shaping up.

★ ★ ★ ★ ★ **You:** I'm sure I can help with that. In my last job, the group I managed had people from three different departments that had recently been merged into one. Within a couple of weeks, I personally met with each individual, analyzed the group results, and shared my assessment with my boss.

If this is an important topic, the dialogue may continue on for a few more exchanges. That will depend on the question. The goal is to get in touch with the interviewer's needs and to demonstrate that you can help. By using this "Five-Star Interview Model," the bar is definitely raised on how much you will learn. But the real keys are engaging the interviewer and getting aligned with the prospective company's needs.

# Your Interviewing "Achilles Heel": Everyone Has One

CONVENTIONAL WISDOM: If you have a problem in your background, do your best to keep it from being a topic of conversation in an interview.

NEW THINKING: Be prepared to respond to questions about issues in your background—and when appropriate bring the issue to light and diffuse it.

*Achilles:*

*In Greek mythology, Achilles was the principal hero of the Trojan War. He was dipped in the River Styx as a baby by his mother and was made invulnerable, except for the heel she held him by.*

*Achilles' Heel:*

*A weakness that seems small but makes somebody or something fatally vulnerable.*

What is the weakness in your career background that could potentially give you the most trouble in an interview? Your "Achilles' heel" may be lack of a college degree, a poor reference from your most recent job, frequent job changes, out-of-date technical skills, or (even though it's illegal to take it into consideration) your age.

# First Things First: Own Your Issue

Don't ignore the issue. Identify what has given you trouble in past interviews or, if the issue is relatively new, identify the issue you know needs to be handled. Write down potential questions that may be asked. For example, if you have had three jobs in the past four years, the question asked may be something along the lines of, "Please explain your frequent job changes."

# The Best Defense is a Good Offense

In preparation for your interview, think through how you will address the issue.

1. *State (or restate) the issue:* "I understand your concern (or you may be concerned that) I have had three jobs in the past four years."

2. *Provide a reason:* "This economy has been difficult for many businesses. In my last two jobs, one of the companies I worked for went out of business. The other one downsized over 50%, and my position was eliminated."

3. *Provide a positive spin:*

    a. Option #1: "I consider myself fortunate to have the skills to be continuously employed during this time, compared to many of my friends who have not been able to find work."

    b. Option #2: "Being at each of these different companies has given me a lot of experience and perspective that I would not have gotten otherwise. I'm looking forward to applying this experience to my next position."

# Beware the Elephant in the Room

What about situations where there's an obvious problem area, but the interviewer doesn't bring it up? You may need to be proactive in addressing it. These unacknowledged concerns, like "the elephant in the room," aren't going away and could be detrimental to your chances for an offer.

Sales people know that just because a customer doesn't mention an objection, it doesn't mean there isn't one. In fact, sales people spend a lot of time ferretting out the objections so that they can be dealt with rather than become deal breakers. It's the same with interviews. If you don't have a chance to deal with the problem area, then you also don't have an opportunity to diffuse it. You may not assuage the interviewer, but at least you have given it your best shot.

Everyone has an interviewing Achilles' heel, whether you talk about it or not. Be sure you identify and craft good answers to potential questions and have a plan for addressing problem areas.

# Happy Endings

**CONVENTIONAL WISDOM:** Being poised and able to think quickly on your feet is all that is required to have a good interview.

**NEW THINKING:** 95% of a successful interview happens before you walk in the door.

Here's a fact. The person who gets hired is not going to be the person with the best resume, the person with the best contacts, or even the person with the best experience. It will be the person who interviews best.

## The Key? Preparation

In our experience, at least 75% of a person's interview success comes from preparation. Another 20% of success in an interview comes from poise and confidence. That means a mere 5% comes from on-the-spot performance. The interesting corollary is that when a person invests time and energy in preparing for the interview, it increases their confidence. *Voila!* Better odds for success.

Over the years, we've developed an interview preparation model that really works. It consists of seven simple steps outlined below. While the steps are straightforward, it does take time and thought to do the work. So don't wait until the day before your big interview to get the job done. The good news is that when you're prepared for one interview, you've got the basics ready for almost every interview thereafter. We recommend compiling your notes, scripts, and facts into an Interview Journal or file you can modify, build on, and refer back to throughout your career.

# Seven Steps to a Killer Interview

### *Interview Preparation Step 1. Prepare Your "About Me" Statement.*

Over 70% of recruiters and hiring managers report that they ask, "Tell me about yourself." That being the case, there is no excuse for not having a succinct and compelling answer to this question on the tip of your tongue. Keep your answer centered around your education, work experience, and your best assets that relate to the job you are interviewing for.

If you want or need more help in how to introduce yourself be sure to read our book, *Be Sharp*, which discusses introductions at length.

### *Interview Preparation Step 2. Identify Your Assets.*

This may seem like a no-brainer, but many of us simply don't recognize all of our own assets. To get you started on your list of assets, study your resume (yes, study your own resume!) and write down a list of your assets. You can also do a flash writing exercise. Write as many talents and skills you possess that you can think of within two minutes. Set the timer for two minutes again, but this time complete this sentence: "I am…" with as many positive attributes or adjectives you can think of. Make sure you only use words with positive connotations.

Next take the lists you've made and select the five or six you are most proud of that are aligned with the targeted job requirements. Construct supporting statements using these selections. Make them strong, bold, and active and with enough substance to be compelling. The basic construct for these statements is:

I demonstrated my _____ when I _____.

For example, let's say you demonstrated your "leadership" when you "led my team to #1 in the district with 35% conversion. I did this by sharing my goal to be #1 with everyone on the team and by encouraging them to be a part of the solution."

Don't be tentative or self-effacing. Be bold and active in your statements.

### *Interview Preparation Step 3. Know Your "Achilles' Heel."*

There is nothing worse than not having a good answer to a negative question. Be prepared to answer them. Here's how to make sure you nail these questions.

Identify the one or two weakest parts of your resume, background, or experience. Then craft some potential questions you could be asked, based on these weaknesses. Practice answering them. When answering the questions, be candid and authentic. Be prepared with a logical and appropriate response that puts you in the best light. If something negative happened, show how you turned it around, transforming it into a positive overall experience.

Be prepared for these common questions:

- ▸ What's your greatest weakness?
- ▸ What regrets do you have?
- ▸ What mistakes have you made?
- ▸ If you could have a do-over, what would it be?

When you answer these questions, stick with business and work-related answers and avoid anything personal. It's safer to choose things that happened early on in your career. And always end on a positive note. Share what you learned, what was good about it, and how it shaped who you are. Always make it a happy ending!

Remember to write down your answers to these questions and keep it in your interview file.

### *Interview Preparation Step 4. Prepare 5 to 8 Scenarios.*

Be sure to have prepped answers for the type of questions you expect to be asked.

Prepare your answers by giving the background and stating the problem that was encountered (if any). When answering the question, share what you did, how you handled the situation, and why the outcome was positive. Always focus on the positive result, especially if what occurred was negative. Share what you learned, whether you created a new process or approach, and again, always end with a happy ending. Life happens, business happens—it's what you do with it that counts.

### *Interview Preparation Step 5. Do Your Research.*

In order to be properly prepared for the interview, find out everything you can about the role, the company, the unit you'll be working with, the people, and the hiring manager. Make a list of questions you would like to know the answers to: major needs, challenges, risks, the company's reputation, competition, and culture. Try to find these answers through research.

You can find some of this information from formal sources: the job description or posting; company material like annual reports, company website or brochures; industry publications and directories; S&P Register of Corporation Directors and Executives; Wall Street analyst reports; and the public relations department. The Internet is also a rich source for research. In particular, Wikipedia has become a robust and rapidly expanding source of company and industry information. Plus more and more companies are creating company profiles on LinkedIn. You can also tap informal sources such as current and former employees, colleagues, competitors, suppliers, customers, recruiters, or even the corporate receptionist.

### *Interview Preparation Step 6. Prepare 5 to 6 Questions Ahead of Time to Ask the Interviewer.*

When the interviewer asks you if you have any questions, your answer must be "yes." Be sure to have several questions prepared ahead of time. It's fine to refer to your notes during this portion of the interview.

Just remember that the questions you ask should not concern the pay rate or any personal concerns or issues you may have. Instead, focus on questions that show your critical thinking ability. They should demonstrate you are insightful and adept at current topics and should show how you think, how you approach your job, and how you can contribute.

### *Interview Preparation Step 7. Practice, Practice, Practice.*

Now that you have all your questions and statements prepared, practice using them with a friend or coach. Create and maintain your Interview Journal, where you can keep track of good answers when you come up with them or hear them from others. It's also where you can record and develop answers for questions you weren't prepared for.

We suggest that clients incorporate a Post Interview Debrief in their Interview Journal. You can use a simple form that records your evaluation of your strengths, difficulties or challenges, ability to engage the interviewer, and recommendations "to self" for improvement in future interviews. This can also be a handy tool for managing follow up items from the interview, such as thank you notes, documents you need to forward, and other key activities related to this company and this job.

Finally, if you're particularly interested in a specific job, try not to have that be the first interview you go on. Instead, take several "practice" interviews if possible.

# Interviewing Dos and Don'ts

*First, the "Dos"*

▸ When preparing your answers, make sure they are no more than two minutes. Get to the point. Give crisp and concise answers.

▸ Answer the question. Then explain or elaborate. Instead of saying "yes" or "no," be sure to give an example. A good rule of thumb is to give at least a 30-second answer.

▸ Let the interviewer "double click." If the interviewer wants something more specific, he or she will probe. If you feel they want something more it is okay to ask, "Did that adequately answer your question?" or "Would you like more information?" They will follow up on what they are most interested in.

▸ Don't just talk. Try to have a "talking" balance. The interview should be a dialogue, not a monologue.

▸ It's okay to pause to think before you answer.

▸ It's okay to ask for clarification.

*Now, the "Don'ts"*

▸ NEVER bring up money—there's a time and way to deal with compensation.

▸ NEVER speak badly about your former company or boss.

▸ NEVER lie: Spin—YES, Lie—NO.

▸ NEVER show up late.

▸ NEVER fail to have extra resumes, bios, and business cards on hand.

▸ NEVER forget to send thank you notes.

▸ NEVER say "no" to the job during an interview. Stay in the game. If you don't get an offer, you don't have a chance to turn it down or negotiate.

Interviewing is like the old television show "The Dating Game." You want the interviewer to fall in love with you. Convince them you are the best candidate.

With some diligent and thoughtful preparation, you can celebrate a happy ending to a successful job search.

## Keys to Powerful and Effective Interview Scenarios

Good interview preparation includes 5-8 scenarios. With just a few well thought-out and carefully crafted stories, you can answer just about any behavioral interview question they can come up with. Choose several situations in which you were particularly proud of your performance and results. Maybe you won an award, received public acknowledgment, or even got a promotion as a result. These "stories" can come right from your resume accomplishments, or they might come from performance reviews or personal recommendations.

A few (2-3) of your scenarios need to be "negative" ones—experiences where the project did not go as planned, the decision was a poor one, the result was disappointing for some reason. The way you handle a negative outcome can show the hiring manager a lot about your character, your sense of responsibility, your courage, and your problem solving ability. Your candor and transparency could make all the difference between getting the offer and finishing in second place.

Complete the first three parts for every interview scenario you prepare. Then also complete parts four and five for negative scenarios

**Part 1. Problem or issue description.** Briefly share the background of the situation or issue. What was the problem? Why was it an issue? What was your role or responsibility in the circumstances? Be concise and keep the details to the minimum necessary to set up the back story.

**Part 2. What you did.** Describe what actions you took and how you came to those decisions. Emphasize the decision making process. Indicate how you overcame any obstacles or barriers. Even if the situation was a team endeavor, the focus is on your actions and your contributions.

**Part 3. Outcome or results.** Summarize the positive (or negative) outcome from your efforts or decisions. Include quantifiable data if possible.

□ □ □

If this scenario is a "negative" one, then you must include the next two parts.

**Part 4. What you did to fix it.** If the project was a bust or you had to reverse a decision you made, then indicate what steps you took to make it right and get back on track—with your customers, your employees, your boss, whoever was impacted by the outcome. Describe how your took responsibility and how you delivered a new and improved outcome.

**Part 5. What you learned from the experience.** We all make mistakes—no one is perfect. But you shouldn't have to learn the same lesson over and over. In an interview, you want to assure the hiring manager that you have learned an important lesson from the situation that you won't have to learn again. To cap off the happy ending, you should summarize a new process or tool that you adopted to ensure your success in similar situations in the future.

# Cutting Through the Confusion about Illegal Questions

> **CONVENTIONAL WISDOM**: There are lots of things that interviewers aren't supposed to ask but for the average interviewee it's still going to be stressful to figure out whether a question is illegal and if so, what to do about it.
>
> **NEW THINKING**: Identifying illegal questions is straightforward and handling them just takes a little finesse.

Most illegal questions are not intentional or malicious. Most are asked innocently by an unsophisticated, untrained interviewer. Common areas for missteps are age, availability for work and travel, birthplace and citizenship, clubs and affiliations, disabilities, economic status, name (e.g. name change, maiden name), family planning, and relatives. Knowing this, you can deal with them from the perspective that a question is fine if it is job-related and illegal if it's not.

Also, interviewers have to be consistent in asking questions across the board, not singling out particular classes of candidates—for example only women. What often happens is that a well-intentioned interviewer asks a "surrogate" question that is based on faulty assumptions.

For example, they might ask a woman, "Are you married?" as a surrogate for "Will you travel out-of-town?"

# Sample Situations

*Situation:* The employer would like someone who speaks Spanish because many of its customers speak Spanish.

*Job-related legal question:* Do you speak Spanish? How well?—Fluent or conversational?

*Illegal question:* What languages do you speak? (If you happen to speak Mandarin Chinese, not only is it irrelevant but might be the cause for bias.)

*Situation:* The job requires overtime, sometimes on short notice

*Job-related legal question:* Are there any circumstances that would prevent you from working overtime on short notice?

*Illegal question:* Do you have children under the age of 10? (First of all, it's unlikely that this would ever be job-related. Secondly, do you think they ask this question to the men too? And by the way, for all the interviewer knows, the woman may be the breadwinner and the husband the children's primary caretaker.)

Some companies provide interviewers with structured questionnaires to guide them. This helps generate legal questions and establishes a consistent interview process for multiple candidates, reducing potential claims of discrimination. In other companies, it is a free-for-all.

# What Can You Do?

1.  You can aggravate the interviewers. You can confront the fact that they asked an illegal question and pretty much guarantee that you won't get the job.

2.  You can answer the question. It may not be the place to make a mountain out of a mole hill. If it doesn't seem like a big issue, why not just answer the question. On the other hand, you don't have to.

3.  You can finesse the question. Figure out what the interviewer is actually trying to find out and redirect your answer to address the job requirement. For example, if you are asked, do you have children, you might say I'm fully prepared for the responsibilities for this job and do not have other responsibilities that would interfere with my work.

4.  You can turn the question around to the interviewer. Rather than dodge the question or irritate the interviewer, you might inquire politely how the topic is related to the job requirements.

Handling illegal questions "real time" can be challenging, but if you keep the overriding principle in mind—how is it job related—you will be fine.

# Not All Advice Is Good Advice

---

**CONVENTIONAL WISDOM**: Anyone who is in the business of helping people get hired has good advice.

**NEW THINKING**: There is a lot of bad advice out there.

---

We are astounded how much bad career advice there is out there, even from sources you would expect to be authoritative. In particular, be wary of adopting career advice published online where it's easy for anyone to position themselves as an expert.

The example below is a blog post with career advice that a client recently forwarded to us. The author suggested three questions for interviewers to use, then suggested the "correct" answers and explained why. In our opinion, this might be the most mind-blowing example of bad advice we have seen.

It was posted by a "diversified search and placement firm focused on sales and marketing executives within the financial services industry." The firm says it offers "a complete recruiting strategy through competitive intelligence, industry relationships, in-depth research, and strategic planning."

# Original Posting, Exactly As It Appeared

## *Three Great Job Interview Questions*

*Everyone has heard the standard interview questions. Why do you want to work for this company? What motivates you? What is your greatest strength? The problem with these questions is that everyone has a standard answer. Asking non-traditional, possibly silly questions can provide insight into an individual's intellect, background, and motivation.*

Q. Ask a candidate what their parents or siblings do for a living?

A. It is not uncommon for an individual to follow the same career path as their parents or siblings. Although this is not always the case, one could argue that success breed's success.

Q. Does the candidate do his/her own taxes?

A. This question appears on several personality tests that candidates often take after finishing the interview process. The idea is that an individual that uses someone else to help them complete their own taxes values the insight of others and is more adept to being a team player.

Q. Ask the candidate why are city street manhole covers round?

A. This is a question that Microsoft is notorious for asking throughout their interview process. The answer is twofold. Manhole covers are round so that they have no way of falling into the manhole. In addition, a manhole cover is round because it is easier to move (it can be rolled rather than having to pick it up). Anyone who can answer this question knows how to think on their feet!

# Our Posted Comments

*While your information is interesting, these are poor, not great, questions. They reflect assumptions that are unsubstantiated and are in some cases illegal. To be a legal interviewing question, it must be JOB related. Asking a candidate what parents or siblings do for a living is one of the most obvious of all of illegal questions. Candidates should be taught how to recognize these questions and how to respond to them specifically in terms of job requirements.*

*Regarding doing their own taxes, regardless of how many "personality" tests this shows up on, the assumption that having someone else do them is a measure of anything is absurd. There are numerous examples of people who do their own taxes and also value the insight of others and are team players—they are just smart enough about doing taxes, especially with all of the currently available software, that they carefully consider the calculus of time and money to do it themselves and make an informed decision. Moreover, this question flirts too close to the boundaries of legality by delving inappropriately into the candidate's personal life. If anything, the question should be "how do you determine whether or not to do your own taxes," which could provide insight into the person's decision-making process, which is often job related. That way the candidate is not required to reveal anything inappropriately personal - although still be cautious because the candidate may interpret it as requiring disclosure of what they actually do.*

*And finally, yes, the "manhole" question has been around for a long time. It's interesting but frankly irrelevant—how you handle a question for which you do not know the answer is more important than getting the answer right. Good interviewers should be interested in how a candidate thinks, makes decision, and acts—not having the right answer to a trick or illegal question. This can be more effectively determined by an interviewer skilled in behavioral interviewing using fully legal and job related questions.*

Need we say more?

# An Interview Is Not a Consulting Gig

**CONVENTIONAL WISDOM**: Don't comply at your own peril. Interviewers hold all the cards.

**NEW THINKING**: You don't have to "give it away" to get the job.

Picking your brain is a common interviewing technique of some companies. In the name of the interviewing process, they ask candidates for solutions to specific issues, plans for what they would do if they were selected for the job, or even comprehensive strategy evaluations.

We had one client who made the slate for a senior executive role and was asked by the company to provide this type of information. She shared with us, after the fact, that she had provided it. The information took her many hours to compile and was delivered in a 20-page report. Guess what? She didn't get the job. They eventually selected another candidate but in the meantime collected free consulting from everyone else. Frankly, even if it were a reasonable request, as a candidate you simply don't know enough about the company, the culture, the people, or the issues to provide such plans and appropriate guidance anyway.

Another client, a sales executive, was asked to provide a list of his top contacts in the market, ostensibly to prove his credibility and to demonstrate that he would be able bring in a book of business and quickly generate revenues for the new company. Wisely, he chose not to do this—and landed the job anyway. The company had other ways, for example talking with references, to evaluate this candidate's capabilities.

# Setting Boundaries

Many candidates assume they have to comply with such requests if they want to be seriously considered. That's not true.

When a request from an organization feels like a consulting gig or a request for your assets without compensation, the request is probably over the line. It's that simple.

So how do you stay in the game without giving away your consulting services, your contact database, prior company confidential information, your intellectual property, or your valuable time? After all, you want the job. But you also want to make sure the price you pay isn't too steep.

The key to an appropriate response is to say "no" but provide an acceptable option for satisfying the underlying objective.

*Request for Contacts:* This is an easy one. *No.* You are happy to provide references (who, by the way, are prepared to accept a call on your behalf). These key people can validate your skills and abilities in building and maintaining a relevant professional network.

*Company Confidential Information:* This is also easy. *No.* The key here is to handle this request gracefully but firmly. A good response is, "Unfortunately, this is confidential information, and I'm not at liberty to share it." End of conversation. If you are pressed further, rinse and repeat. You never know—this may be a test about how you handle confidential information.

***Intellectual Property:*** This request is a bit more complicated. There is a range of appropriate and reasonable responses. There are certain items, like a published book or anything that can be accessed in the public domain, which you can give to them. At the other extreme, you may have proprietary models, formulas, or solutions that you are not willing to disclose at this stage of the conversation. In the latter situation, your response should indicate that you would be willing to negotiate how this information would be shared upon being hired. Somewhere in the middle of these two extremes are your "work products," like training manuals, presentations, or creative portfolio materials. Your response here might be to offer a "show and tell" session, but we recommend you do not provide your materials in advance or leave them behind. It's your choice, of course, but we invite you to consider what your intellectual property is worth.

***Presentations:*** If your targeted job requires an element of speaking, training, or "performance," you may be requested to make a presentation. This is most likely a test of skill and would be a perfectly appropriate request. You should be happy to comply. Be sure you're clear, however, about whether the purpose of the presentation is to measure your skills or to acquire your content.

***Consulting Services:*** This area is very muddy. On the one hand, you need to provide enough qualitative information to validate your competence. However, at some point what you provide may cross the line into "free consulting." Where this line is drawn is a judgment call. Consider these criteria:

- ▸ Is the output a document or a conversation?
- ▸ Can this be done quickly, or is this a major project?
- ▸ Is it an overview or a comprehensive evaluation?
- ▸ Are they asking for approaches or calling for solutions?

> ▸ Does it require unique knowledge or expertise that a non-employee would not have?
>
> ▸ Is the question hypothetical or a real issue the company is dealing with?

For example, let's say you are an IT executive, and you are interviewing for a Director of Applications Development position. As part of the interview process, the company shares that they are considering implementing a global cloud computing strategy. In one instance, they ask you to provide a comprehensive comparison and evaluation of three different solutions they are considering. In this instance, they are actually asking you for free consulting. Your answer is "no." You can explain that there are far too many factors and environmental considerations unknown to you to provide this level of evaluation.

On the other hand, the company might ask a behavioral interviewing question like, "Tell me about a time when you evaluated competing infrastructure solutions that would have global impact on the business." This question explores your prior performance and actual experience in making these kinds of decisions. Another way the company might approach this issue would be to ask, "How would you go about designing a cloud computing strategy?" This question invites you to comment on your thought process and decision making approach. In either of these situations, you want to be as forthcoming and thorough as possible when answering the question.

The bottom line is that in any interviewing situation, you have an opportunity to legitimately assess the reasonableness of the request. Just because they say "jump," you don't have to say "how high?" Value what you are bringing to the table. As long as you remain professional, you can say "no" to unreasonable requests and stay in the game. It some cases, it could win you the job.

# References Are Assets—
# Don't Squander Them

CONVENTIONAL WISDOM: Put a list of contacts on your resume or have a sheet of your references on hand to give to an interviewer.

NEW THINKING: Have several names in mind of people for interviewers to call but only provide them later, after the interview.

**M**any companies are required to get references, and the basic forms you fill out, especially when you apply online, require you to list them. Always have three references who have given you permission to put them on every application you fill out. To that end, always make sure these references are solid. These people should know they are on the list and be prepared for a call and should also be aware of what jobs and companies you are applying to.

## Tailored References—and One Person Not on Your List

For college graduates and higher level management where there are usually multiple interviews, references are typically requested at the second or third interview. Instead of using your basic list, you'll want to provide the interviewer with a well thought out group of references. At this point you'll know more about the company and the job and will be able to customize your references according to those who can best represent you for the particular job. You'll want to choose references who can speak to how your qualifications meet the needs of both the job and the organization. If you know someone who has ties to the organization or the industry, and that person can honestly assess you, he or she could be a powerful reference.

Unless there are special circumstances, one person who should not be on your list of references is your current supervisor. It's normally inappropriate for the recruiter to call the company at which you are currently working for a reference. If an interviewer asks if they can contact your current supervisor, you should feel free to say "no."

## Where and When

Most people know enough not to list references directly on their resumes. However, we still see plenty of job seekers who include the line "references available upon request." Well, duh. Of course your references are available upon request. This is an obsolete appendage from an earlier era.

At some point, when a company is seriously interested in you, they will ask you for references. Do not whip out a page with prepared references. Instead, let the interviewer know you'll be happy to provide references and arrange to provide a list the next morning.

Why? During the job search, references are one of your greatest assets and need to be treated carefully and with respect. You'll want to give careful consideration to both the job and the company and choose the references who will speak best for you in that particular circumstance. You'll also want a little time to call the reference to let them know they will be contacted and to discuss the job with them so they will take the call and be prepared to talk about you. Ideally, this gives you a chance to know what they are going to say about you. Furthermore, you don't want your reference to be on a month-long vacation in Hong Kong when your potential employer calls. And, from time to time, someone might prefer not to be a reference for that job or company, and you are giving them the opportunity to decline. You don't want to put them in an awkward position or worse, have them give you a bad reference.

Think of your references as gold. Don't squander them by listing them on your resume or giving them out prematurely. With a little preparation, you can ensure your recommendations are tailored to your situation and do what they are supposed to do—help you get the job.

# ABOUT MONEY:

# OFFER NEGOTIATION AND COMPENSATION

# ♫ Money, Money, Money, Mon-ey . . . MON-EY! ♫

CONVENTIONAL WISDOM: If somebody asks you about your salary expectations, give them a number.

NEW THINKING: If someone asks you about your salary expectations, do NOT give them a number.

Talking about money in the interview process is a tricky matter. It's one of those areas where you can do more harm than good. On the one hand, you want to stay in the race, get through the early screening process, get the interview, and then ultimately get the job offer. Even if the offer isn't what you want or need at the outset, you can usually negotiate something more attractive or you can turn it down. Bottom line, if you don't get an interview, you'll never get the job offer. And if you don't get an offer, you'll never have a chance to see if the company can make the economics work for you.

On the other hand, how do you know if the job is something you want or if you can get paid what you deserve if you don't talk about money? Interviewers, especially in the screening process, will almost always ask about money. They need to confirm early on whether you are in the range and are therefore "qualified" to move forward. What's the harm with telling them your target salary? They expect it, don't they? All too aften candidates just blurt out a number.

The reality is that as soon as you give an interviewer a number, you have potentially put yourself at a disadvantage. The odds are infinitesimally low that you'll hit the budgeted salary spot on. You may get lucky, but you're more likely to get one of the two following outcomes: 1) you give a dollar amount that the screener thinks is too high, and your prospects for moving forward in the process are nipped in the bud; or 2) you give them an amount that's too low, and you've set the ceiling on the amount of the offer they will eventually give you. Either way, you've undermined your potential and "bid against yourself." You risk disqualifying yourself or leaving money on the table.

There is an important overarching assumption to keep in mind when you consider the discussions about money. Basically, if the job scope and content seem to fit what you are interested in and qualified to perform, then the law of market forces should result in a compensation structure that is competitive and appropriate. So don't get too hung up on money before you've had a chance to get more information and also present yourself in the best light.

There are also two important interviewing principles that apply. First, "practice makes perfect." Try to stay in the game for as long as you can, even if it's just to get more experience interviewing. Of course, there may be some opportunities where the job is obviously not a good fit or other factors would cause you to decide early on that you would not accept an offer even if they gave you one. Also, out of integrity and respect for the process, you may determine that withdrawing from the competition is the right thing to do for a number of reasons. However, we would encourage you to keep an open mind and be careful of making negative assumptions prematurely. Further, you might be able to be authentic and transparent with your interviewers while continuing the discussions at some level. Who knows, they could decide to change the job specifications once they get to know you!

Second, the people you talk with in the interviewing process become new networking contacts for you. If you have good chemistry or have some things in common, they can be added to your growing network of professional resources. If you take the job, you've got new allies in the company. If you don't win the job, you still have resources for further networking. Remember to get their business cards, add them to your contact database, and invite them to connect on LinkedIn immediately.

## How the Question Is Asked Makes the Difference

Fundamentally, there are two different ways an interviewer will ask you about money.

The most common questions are like these:

- ► "How much do you expect to get paid for this job?"
- ► "What are your salary expectations?"
- ► "What compensation are you looking for?"

Basically, it is usually a screener who is asking this question, and they just want to confirm that the money you expect to receive is in the ballpark of what they are willing to pay. It's their job to "qualify the candidates" and not put someone through to the next step that doesn't fit the profile.

The answer to this form of the question is to *not* give them a number—not even a range if you can possibly avoid it. Don't be tempted. Yes, it's easier to say the number, but don't do it.

The "right" answer to this question is to get qualified by saying something like, "Based on my understanding of this job, the responsibilities, and scope, I'm confident a competitive compensation package (or salary) will be fine." Another way to respond would be "I am expecting a market compensation that reflects the responsibilities and requirements of this role." If the screener will leave it there, great. Say no more. But some interviewers will probe further. If they continue to press for a number, and you're pretty sure they won't give up, turn it around and ask them, diplomatically of course, "What is the targeted range for this job?" Unless the range is just ridiculous, say something like, "I'm comfortable with that range." Also, just a side note: if the range is absurd, then there must be something you don't understand about the job. Ask for clarification.

A less common—but more insightful way—the question is asked, is:

- ▶ "What are you currently making?"
- ▶ "How much did you make in your last job?"

In this way, they are asking for actual facts and data, not speculation. You will come across as flaky or worse, suspicious, if you try to dodge this form of the question. So in this situation, you really do have to give them a number. But there are some subtle factors to consider in how you answer. In most cases, you want to address the complete economics of your compensation from a competitive, comparative point of view. It's not just about your base salary but includes such things as bonuses, commissions, awards, when you are due for a raise, and unusually generous benefits.

If you have received bonuses or commissions, you can provide your "total cash compensation." Hint: Take a look at your W-2, Box 2. If these have varied widely over the last few years, then you can give them your "average cash compensation" for the last few years. You want to fairly represent your income even when the most current year may not have been your best. In addition, if you have received other meaningful economic benefits, add them to the response. "In addition, I have (or had) a company car provided; " or "My prior company also provided an exceptional 401(k) matching of 10%;" or "All my medical and disability premiums for my entire family were paid by the company." Don't you wish? You don't need to mention employee benefits that are standard in the industry or normal for the position. In fact, screeners can be annoyed when candidates include standard types of benefits that appear to inflate compensation. If you can quantify the economic value of "super benefits," then you might consider providing that number. For example, "My company car plan was worth approximately $14,000 annually over and above my cash compensation."

## Tricky Situations

There are three circumstances that may be a bit more complicated and require more finesse.

First, if you're a new graduate you obviously don't have a "real" number. You may have been a server, cashier, or clerk, and your income in those jobs is not relevant to your new opportunity. When you are asked, "What were you making in your last job?" let them know, or remind them, that you are a new graduate and you are confident that the market range for the position will be suitable.

Second, in some rare but real situations, you may have made a lot more in your prior job than you expect to be paid in the job being considered. There are several reasons this could happen. You could have received a massive "stay-on" bonus during a company restructuring or acquisition. You might be drastically changing your career direction and are willing to take a step backward from a compensation perspective to reposition yourself in a new role. In these situations, you may have to give them the number but immediately add the caveat that you are fully aware that the job you are being considered for is not in that range, and that you are absolutely committed to making the shift. Your goal in this situation is to convince the recruiter to give you a chance. Otherwise, game over before you even start the discussions.

Third, you may be currently underpaid relative to the market for various reasons. For example, your company may have had salary freezes in place for an extended period of time due to restructuring, financial trouble, divestitures, lay-offs, and regulatory constraints. In these cases, you may have to provide your current salary but immediately comment that you know your compensation is below market for your job and qualifications. You should be careful not to add information that in any way disrespects your current company or shares any information that is confidential.

# Screening Is Not Negotiating

These early discussions about money are all about getting qualified so you remain a contender in the race. Once you have made it past this hurdle, the topic will often be tabled and not resurrected until they are ready to make a job offer. Let's assume you have made it through the gauntlet and succeeded in the "dating game" of interviewing, and they have finally decided that you are "the one." They are in love, and you win the prize. Now the power shifts to you. Until this moment in time, the company held all the power. You were one of several being considered, and at any time they could have chosen someone else. But now, you are their #1 choice. You're negotiating now, not being screened anymore.

Whatever offer they make, you always have the option to make a counteroffer. Of course, if the offer blows your socks off, you might want to just say, "Yes. When do you want me to start?" However, this doesn't happen that often, so the first thing to do is buy a little time to get your ducks in a row. Thank them for the offer and indicate you would like to think about it. Always keep "selling" yourself right to the end. "I'm excited about the opportunity, and I'm confident that I can be a strong asset for your team."

Don't be afraid to ask for more money. Sometimes you can ask for stock or a sign-on bonus to compensate you for something you are leaving behind. What about more vacation days? If they can't add more money immediately, you may be able to negotiate a six-month review and salary adjustment at that time. Standard benefit packages such as insurance or 401(k) are not usually negotiable, so you have to fully consider the total economics of the deal you are being offered. When the company accepts your final offer, you are fairly certain you didn't leave too much on the table.

At the end of the day, if they make you a lousy offer and they are not willing to negotiate something you can live with, you can always turn it down. But you don't even get that chance if you don't make it through the first round of screening.

# Role of Recruiter in Negotiations

CONVENTIONAL WISDOM: Even if you are working with an external executive recruiter, you are likely to do better if you negotiate your compensation directly with the hiring executive.

NEW THINKING: Whenever you are working with an external executive recruiter, use that relationship to its fullest benefit to negotiate compensation that ends up in a job offer.

Q. When is the recruiter your BFF?

A. In compensation negotiations when everyone wants the deal to close.

One of the key roles of an executive search recruiter—a recruiter who is paid for the recruiting engagement regardless of the outcome—is to serve as an intermediary in negotiating compensation and the job offer. When you work with contingency recruiters, those who get paid only for placements, some will take on the role of intermediary, and others will merely pass the company's offer to you. Ultimately, negotiating your compensation package in these cases will probably fall to you. You will still want to take advantage of the knowledge and experience that the contingency recruiter can provide.

When the recruiter is functioning as an effective intermediary, the goal is for a company to present an offer they are certain the candidate of choice will accept. For a good candidate, the recruiter may be able to convince the company to improve their offer. For an unrealistic candidate, they may be able to provide perspective on what is being offered. Companies do not like to engage in frustrating discussions or be put in a position where members of the hiring team inadvertently (or on purpose) sabotage the company's employment practices and create ancillary problems. Most importantly, they hate being boxed into a corner or turned down after they are invested in their selection.

## Recruiters as Skilled Mediators

Most executive recruiters have intimate knowledge of the company, the personalities and egos, the sensitivities, the compensation structures, and the job requirements. They also know the limits to which a company will stretch, have determined what the candidate wants, and understands the market for similar talent. They are frequently skilled mediators, having been through this process with many clients and many candidates over the years. The executive recruiter provides a safe environment where each party can be open about their interests. Most often, the recruiter works with the company and the candidate, sometimes through several rounds of negotiation, to create a solution—frequently better than the package the company originally anticipated—and to obtain a commitment from both sides. Recruiters are motivated to make successful placements, both for their own reputation and to close the search. In addition, recruiters are unlikely to undermine the candidate's compensation, as it is frequently a key factor in their own fees.

## The Hazards of Direct Negotiation

If you go around the recruiter and attempt to negotiate directly with the company representative or with the hiring manager or executive, it may work. The smallest downside is that everyone except you and the person you finally negotiate with is unhappy. And this unhappiness may follow you in ways you don't imagine or possibly ever know about. The biggest downside is that the company has a sophisticated hiring process and chooses not to hire you after all, either because they find your behavior inappropriate (after all, they hired the recruiter in the first place because they don't want you bothering them) or because the negotiation process goes badly.

Here's a perfect example. A recruiter found a well-qualified candidate, and the company was interested in hiring the person. In order to successfully negotiate an offer, the company needed to sweeten the pot with additional relocation expense funds and a small increase in compensation to meet the market value of a person of this quality. The candidate had unrealistic expectations of the compensation package and had several demands that the company was not willing to meet. The candidate elected to go around not only the executive search recruiter but also the company's HR representative, directly to the hiring executive. The hiring executive was annoyed, the HR representative lost face, and the recruiting firm was embarrassed by the candidate's behavior. The company eventually stonewalled any further negotiation with or about the candidate, and the offer was never made. The candidate's arrogance and stupidity cost him the job.

So, evaluate the role of the recruiter as best you can, and reframe your negotiation strategy to be inclusive of the recruiter rather than exclusive. Most of the time, this will reap rewards.

# Silly Ways to Spend Your Money

CONVENTIONAL WISDOM: Anything you can do to stand out or gain access to recruiters or hiring executives is a worthwhile investment.

NEW THINKING: Carefully consider the ROI of your investment. Take into account the real-world behavior of your audience, and beware of services that are more valuable to the seller than to your job search.

Like so many things in life, when you are in the midst of a job search there are many ways to spend your time and money that intuitively seem right but upon further investigation don't hold up. Here are some of the silly ways to spend your money on a job search.

*Resume folders or 9x12 mailing envelopes.* In today's job search world, there are limited times when you will be using a printed resume. Those times will most frequently be when you are meeting someone in person—for networking, an informational interview, or a face-to-face interview. If you do need to give someone your resume discreetly, it can be folded and placed in a standard mailing envelope. We haven't heard of anyone who was removed from consideration for a job because his or her printed resume was folded. Think about what happens in real life to those expensive folders or envelopes. Once the resume is removed, they are immediately discarded directly to the trash can. Why? They obscure the document and don't fit in file folders. So at $0.25 or more for a mailing envelope and $1-2 dollars for a folder, your financial return is better if you buy a lottery ticket.

*Expensive custom business cards.* Yes, impressions matter. Your business cards need to be professional, communicate quality, and get your message across. That does not require custom graphics or printing. Business cards for a job search are not business cards for a business. They are temporary and tactical. In addition, as you progress with your job search, you may want to tweak or even redesign your card to better reflect you or the focus of your search. If you have overinvested in your card, your flexibility is severely limited. There are several Internet companies that allow you to create quality cards quickly using their templates—or customizing them—for less than $25.

*Purchased email blasts.* One of the most popular job search services marketed by career services firms is the "email blast." For a price—usually a hefty price—companies will send an email to a list of contacts. This is the most egregious form of junk mail, bordering on spam. Think about your own experience with email. How much unsolicited email do you actually read? How much do you immediately delete? How much email is filtered out by company firewalls and other security systems? Traditional junk mail has a rate of return ranging from .05—2%, depending upon the likely interest of the target list. For the seller, this is a great service with great margins. You may be charged by the email or a flat rate for a certain number. In any case, these are easy to produce, easy to send, and rarely generate the promised returns.

*Guaranteed job placement.* We just finished reading about what initially seemed to be a legitimate offer from a legitimate firm. Of course, once we read the fine print we realized we were mistaken. In this particular instance you have to be approved (they don't select anyone who isn't a good candidate), the success criteria is one job "offer" (what if you don't want that job), and your compliance with the program (try negotiating whether you were or weren't a good participant). In other cases, they allow you to continue in the program for no cost for another fixed or unlimited term. But if you weren't successful the first time, why would more of the same generate better results? Rather than waste your time and money with one of these programs, take control of your job search and do the hard work of finding your next opportunity. If you need help, there are reputable community-based groups you can join at no cost or qualified career coaches who can guide you professionally.

*Unique, splashy approaches.* Finding unique ways to connect with companies and hiring managers certainly has its place in job searches and is one that should be explored. On the other hand, some examples that make great stories for motivational speakers are usually once-in-a-lifetime successes and frequently have a significant cost. For example, paying the price to send something clever overnight to a senior executive with whom you have no relationship is unlikely to generate job traction. When it comes to being "unique," tread carefully and judiciously.

Overall, you'll want to do whatever you can to go the extra mile and improve your chances of finding a job. However, think carefully about how much it's costing you to stand out. If the service is more valuable to the seller than to you or has a one in a million chance for success, beware.

# Conclusion

With your top-siders and white chinos freshly donned, you step up onto the polished deck of your friend's trusty sailboat. The wind is picking up nicely, and the salt spray tingles your face as you set sail. The bright warm sun reflecting off the water makes the white sails shimmer. What a rush!

You feel the rope's rough surface as you pull the sail tight. The boat leans deeply and groans as it tacks back and forth to the finish line. As the clouds roll in, churning up the waves, and then dissipate, everything you know about sailing is put to a test. Your heart is pounding with effort and excitement. There's just nothing like it.

⚑ ⚑ ⚑

An odd story for a career advice book, huh? Think about how sailing parallels job search and career management.

Successful careers are about strategy, competition, and determination. And your skills and capabilities will assuredly affect the outcome. Will you get to your destination? How quickly? Without incident? There are others in the race with you too.

The incoming wind creates friction and resistance. You can let it push you back or you can harness its power for strong forward momentum.

Careers rarely move in a straight line. You often have to zigzag to keep moving forward. With a strong, clear vision of the end point, you'll get to your destination successfully and enjoy the ride all along the way.

Life is unpredictable—much like the weather. We may think we can predict what is coming our way, but we can be oh-so-wrong. The most successful people know how to handle the unexpected and thrive in the turmoil. Being prepared for all the possibilities is the first step; however, being resourceful and fearless are the most important. You just never know what you might encounter that you didn't plan for. When your boss or company puts a kink in your sail, what you do about it can have powerful and lasting effects.

The exhilaration of the race, or even just the adventure, is satisfying and rewarding. Every minute brings new experiences. Every wave lifts you up and lets you fall. With a smidgen of danger and risk taking, the journey is richer and the ultimate arrival all the more sweet.

Our final words of advice to you are these:

▸ Don't believe all the advice you get from the people around you and even from the "experts." Do your own due diligence.

▸ Challenge assumptions that you or others make about your situation—in your job, your company, your industry, your function. An unemployed client with deep banking experience recently asked us, "Is it reasonable for me to expect to get a job in banking since the industry and the economy are in such bad shape?" Our answer, "If you were looking for 5,000 jobs, that might be problematic, but you only need one. The competition may be tough, but there are plenty of jobs being filled every day. What's it going to take for you to be the best candidate for the job you really want?"

▸ Be open to new thoughts and fresh approaches. The "tried and true" may be outdated.

▸ Seek out wise counsel—talk to "career experts," but always use your own common sense.

We dare you to sail on with gusto, and cherish the ups and downs that come with the journey!

> *Twenty years from now you will be more disappointed by the things that you didn't do than by the ones you did do. So throw off the bowlines. Sail away from the safe harbor. Catch the trade winds in your sails. Explore. Dream. Discover.*
>
> **Mark Twain**

# About the Authors

## Paula Asinof, Principal & Founder

**Yellow Brick Path**
**www.yellowbrickpath.com**

Paula Asinof is the founder of Yellow Brick Path, a career coaching, leadership consulting, and resume services firm. Clients appreciate her straight talk, often unconventional perspectives, and the depth of her "real world" executive experience.

Paula is distinguished by her ability to identify, leverage, and develop talent. Throughout her career, she has helped clients, peers, and subordinates recognize their unique capabilities and position themselves as "A" players by addressing career strategy, leadership development, professional positioning, and visibility. She has a contagious enthusiasm and passionate belief in people that inspires them to become prouder, stronger, and more valuable contributors to their organizations. She has also led innovative initiatives to build top-performing organizations with management "bench strength" and staying power.

Her background includes co-founding Coach Academy International, a cutting-edge accredited coach training program, ten years of Executive Search Recruiting, and serving as Director of a college career services department. Earlier, she held leadership positions in IT and Finance with GTE (now Verizon), Rand McNally, and the Midwest Stock Exchange after beginning her career in public accounting. Paula holds an MBA from The Wharton School, an MA from Columbia University, and a BA from Washington University in St. Louis. She received the prestigious designations of Credentialed Career Manager (CCM) and Master Career Director (MCD) and is an Associate of Career Thought Leaders (CTL). She is also an NLP Practitioner, a Certified NLP Coach (NLPC), and a member of the International Coach Federation (ICF).

Paula is also the co-author of the practical and popular book *Be Sharp: Tell me About Yourself in Great Introductions and Professional Bios*, available on Amazon.com.

## Mina Brown, Founder & President

### Positive Coach LLC
### www.positivecoach.com

Mina Brown is an experienced and insightful executive coach, career consultant, trainer, and popular public speaker. As a former senior operations executive and CFO, she brings together a successful leadership track record and unusual intuition, deep compassion, and unflinching candor.

Mina is widely recognized and sought after for her focus on business and personal strategy and tangible, measurable outcomes. She works with senior executives, executive teams, managers, and high-potential professionals in areas of leadership, influence, conflict, team effectiveness, and career management. She is particularly passionate about supporting professionals at all levels who are changing jobs or changing careers.

Mina is a co-founder of Coach Academy International, a cutting-edge accredited coach training program. Before launching her coaching career, Mina was CFO of Aviall and SVP & General Manager of its Aerospace Division. Earlier, she held corporate management positions with Ryder System and Amax. She started her career with Price Waterhouse.

Mina holds an MBA from Vanderbilt University, a BBA in accounting from Eastern Kentucky University, and a CPA. She is a Board Certified Coach (BCC), Master NLP Practitioner, Certified NLP Coach (NLPC), and one of the early members of the International Coach Federation. She teaches expert coaching to managers and certification candidates in her ICF and BCC accredited program. Mina is a popular keynote speaker and frequent radio and television guest on the topic of careers and leadership.

Mina is also the co-author of the practical and popular book *Be Sharp: "Tell me About Yourself" in Great Introductions and Professional Bios*, available on Amazon.com.

# Be Sharp:
## "Tell Me About Yourself" in Great Introductions and Professional Bios

by Paula Asinof and Mina Brown

*Paperback and Kindle editions available on Amazon*
*Average Customer Reviews* * * * * *

The authors' previous book, *Be Sharp: "Tell Me About Yourself" in Great Introductions and Professional Bios* continues to receive rave reviews. It's a must-read for anyone who needs to introduce themselves smoothly—in an interview, in networking, in sales, and so many other business situations.

# Book Overview

Business today moves fast. And it's unforgiving. When you have an opportunity to meet someone or present yourself for the first time, you create such a lasting impression, good or bad, that it's difficult and maybe impossible to change. Few people have so much personality and self-confidence that they can pull off a flawless personal introduction without preparation or thought.

*Be Sharp* will help you answer the perpetual question "Tell me about yourself" with professional polish and pizzazz. Readers who follow the guidelines will have:

- Engaging, memorable elevator pitch
- Confidence to introduce themselves smoothly anytime anywhere
- Rediscovery and validation of their unique talents and capabilities
- Well thought out introduction for customer meetings, network events, or interviews
- Impressive, high-impact professional bio that gets results
- Know-how to adapt their bio to almost any situation
- Easy, well-honed process for the future

Once you have a solid introduction and your foundation bio, there are numerous ways to use it: job search, business proposals, marketing materials, websites, board bios, service business bios, and public speaking, to name a few. Also, our world of electronic communication demands that you pay attention to your cyberspace presence. This book addresses all these areas.

# Praise for Be Sharp…

"Best Bio and Introduction book around! I am a Career & Personal Branding Strategist who has been asked to write Personal Branding for Dummies. I have been using **BE SHARP** with my clients for the last couple of years and love it. I have recommended it to all of the coaches on a corporate assignment as well. I will be showcasing some of the material in my book."

Susan Chritton, author of *Personal Branding for Dummies*

"**BE SHARP** is a terrific resource for answering that important request "Tell me about yourself." Mina Brown and Paula Asinof provide the definitive approach so you, as a professional, will be prepared for job interviews, career discussions, internal networking, dinner parties, and all those other events that build your career and enrich your life. It is a great read and could potentially change your life."

Susan Bixler, President/CEO of Bixler Consulting Group and author of six books on leadership including *5 Steps to Professional Presence*

"**BE SHARP** is a great hands-on workbook. It is an excellent resource for young professionals and mid-level executives. In particular, it would valuable to those who have been in a single company for a number of years or those who are haven't navigated the job search market recently."

Judy Stubbs, Former Partner, Heidrick & Struggles, one of the world's foremost executive search firms, and Former SVP HR, Mary Kay Cosmetics

"As someone who has been coaching and counseling executives and professionals for twenty years, I am overjoyed to recommend this very practical and relevant book! It is truly the first book I have ever come across devoted to the critical skill of presenting oneself crisply, positively and memorably, both verbally and in writing. **BE SHARP** should be on every career counselor's bookshelf and ought to be required reading for anyone interested in career advancement, whether in transition, aiming for a promotion or eager to make that next sale."

Mark Schor, Ph.D. LPC, Senior Vice President,
Executive Services, Right Management

"This book reminds us to "take care of the basics" to achieve competitive differentiation. How we "show up", especially in these tough times, will certainly make a difference. This can be as simple as how we introduce ourselves, our "elevator pitch", our one page "bio" and "leave behind"...these will make the difference in today's sea of unemployed and/or high potentials looking to achieve greatness! Worth the read—a simple, yet incredibly powerful book of golden nuggets."

Kristin Kaufman, President, Alignment, Inc., and author of
*Is This Seat Taken? Random Encounters That Change Your Life*

"Lots of authors are advising people to create their "brand," but few give you detailed advice on how to approach the task. Here is the book that will help you get the ROI you want from your networking and self-marketing activities. **BE SHARP** gives you both the "why" and the "how" behind creating impactful personal introduction statements, bios, and websites. As experienced executive coaches, the authors also realize the value of producing a personal statement as a means to help you define your professional identity and "market" the identity you want others to recognize."

Nancy Jagmin, President, Jagmin Consulting Group and
Former Vice President of Organizational Capability, Frito-Lay

"In **BE SHARP**, Mina and Paula got it right. You must establish your value and make a solid first impression. In the world of retained executive search we are continually running across candidates that do not make a good first impression, and it is a short interview. If you follow their sound methodology, you will learn how to identify and articulate your value and make that all important positive first impression."

Phil Resch, Partner, Sandhurst Group

"Reading this book was like having a great conversation with Mina and Paula. It made me want to put the book down and take action immediately."

Jeff Crilley, Emmy Award Winning
Journalist and author of *Free Publicity*

"In **BE SHARP**, Paula Asinof and Mina Brown give you the complete turnkey solution to the crucial challenge of creating powerful, positive first impressions. In the lightning-fast pace of today's business, that first impression is quite often your one and only opening to ignite winning relationships and to seize prized opportunities. Yet, the secrets to creating and delivering dynamic personal introductions have never been adequately taught—until NOW! This clear and powerful book will do more than skyrocket your career. It will elevate your confidence and peace of mind in those crucial moments that make the biggest difference in your life."

Brian Biro, America's Breakthrough Coach

"In **BE SHARP**, the authors have given us the most inventive tools I have seen to create the personal marketing materials we need in all aspects of business. The uniquely effective and efficient process takes you on a personal journey in which you will rediscover and reconnect to your most valuable talents and skills. In a few short hours, I was able to communicate my value to the marketplace with authenticity and enthusiasm."

Courtney Q. Shore, SVP, Communications and Marketing

"**BE SHARP** turns a daunting task into an easy to follow, step-by-step process that results in a clear, concise introduction for a powerful first impression."

Mike Johanns, Former Vice President, Supply Chain at Dell

"I've never seen anything like this all in one in place. This is really good! **BE SHARP** offers a concise formula to help any professional powerfully and appropriately let the world know who they are and what they bring to the table in a variety of different circumstances. If you are looking for a leg up on the competition—this could be it."

Chip Lambert, President, Network 2 Networth,
Business Development for the Serious Entrepreneur

"The book is brilliant and concisely written with succinct information relaying information in a readable fashion with interesting examples. The authors' ability to guide structured thinking translates beautifully to capturing the essence of an individual's talents into a superb bio geared for the right market."

Mary Spilman, Managing Partner, Spilman & Associates, Inc.,
Executive Search Consultants

"Powerful, focused advice from people who give outstanding career advice to job seekers every day, on a topic everyone should be an expert—ourselves. Don't even think about meeting anyone new until you've read this book cover to cover."

Steve Purello, Former CEO, Workstream, Inc.,
parent company of 6FigureJobs.com and Allen And Associates

Made in United States
North Haven, CT
22 April 2023

35767717R00137